MW00388061

Cooks & Company

A Collection of Recipes
from Main Street, Indiana

MARIE HUNTINGTON

To Joan,
Wishing you good food, good friend
and good times.

Marie

GUILD PRESS OF INDIANA, INC.

ISBN 1-57860-035-9

Library of Congress
Catalog Card Number
99-73489

Cover and text design by Sheila G. Samson

Printed and bound in the United States of America

Contents

Acknowledgments and Introduction

Shortly after moving to Columbus, Indiana, from the Los Angeles area, I was invited by the Indiana University-Purdue University extension to put together a class demonstrating Chinese cooking. The classes were held in the North Christian Church kitchen, with all the participants cooking, cleaning up, and, of course, eating. One series of classes led to another, and the idea for a shop was born, with the assurance from those first students that they would be supportive of such an endeavor.

I am forever indebted to all the loyal cooking-school enthusiasts who have come to my classes over the past twenty years, as well as to the retail customers who have allowed us to operate a business that has been challenging, but so much fun.

My thanks also to all of the Huntingtons, Yiums, and Tamuras who have given me much encouragement through the years. I owe much appreciation to Larry, my husband, and to Chris, our son, for taste-testing endless recipes, and eating countless leftovers without complaint.

Marie Huntington
September 1999

From the First Lady
of the State of Indiana . . .

Congratulations on the forthcoming cookbook. . . . After twenty years of teaching cooking classes, I'm sure it's satisfying to be able to print [your recipes] in a single collection.

Cooks & Company has been influential in the Columbus community, not only by the services you offer, but also by the rejuvenation it has brought to the downtown area. . . . Businesses such as Cooks & Company are the heart of [Indiana's] Main Street Program. Its owners have invested in the property and work directly in the store, bringing to the community a vested interest in the quality of life in this small town. This collection of recipes from their cooking classes . . . reflects the support the community has given to the business . . . [and is] the perfect opportunity to share your knowledge and hard work with Indiana residents outside of the Columbus community.

Sincerely,
Judy O'Bannon
August 1999

Appetizers

By definition, appetizers are food to stimulate the appetite before a meal. By my own experience, they are designed to satisfy those growling hunger pangs before dinner, and to take the edge off of alcohol that might be served before a meal. Nowadays, many people enjoy making an entire meal of appetizers, and if the food is done well, I can certainly understand how hard it is to eat just one or two.

Appetizers can be the most time-consuming of all the foods we do for catering, but some of our best parties are the ones where the food is served in small portions and passed on a tray. For large parties, that might mean thousands of appetizers!

I'm not sure there are any new hors d'oeuvres, but just new versions or twists on old favorites. I hope you find some new ideas from some of our favorites.

Shrimp Toasts

This classic Chinese appetizer is always a favorite. I usually make them ahead, fry them briefly, drain and then refry just before serving. These can be cooked, frozen, and then reheated in the oven, but they never taste as fresh as when they are fried just prior to serving.

½	pound fresh shrimp
6	slices thin white sandwich bread
1	strip of bacon
8	water chestnuts
2	scallions, finely chopped with some green included
3	tablespoons cornstarch
1	teaspoon salt
2	tablespoons dry sherry
1	small egg, lightly beaten
	Sesame seeds and paprika
4	cups oil

Trim crusts from bread and cut each slice into 4 triangles. Lay bread out on a platter to dry for about 2 hours.

Clean and devein shrimp and mince finely into a pulp-like paste. Chop bacon and water chestnuts until fine. Mix with shrimp, scallions, salt, dry sherry, cornstarch, and beaten egg. Mix well and spread mixture on bread, making a slight mound on each slice. Sprinkle with sesame seeds and paprika and press lightly so they adhere to mixture.

Heat oil in wok or sauté pan. Drop bread, shrimp side down, into oil and fry for 30 seconds. Turn and fry on other side for another 30 seconds. Both sides should be golden brown. Drain on paper towels and serve hot. Makes 24 appetizers.

Chile Cheese Toast

This is delicious with soup. Just toast larger slices for an open-faced sandwich.

	French bread, thinly sliced on the diagonal
1	cup butter, softened
½	cup chopped green chiles
1	clove garlic, minced
½	cup shredded Monterey Jack or Cheddar cheese
1	cup mayonnaise

Toast bread on one side. Combine butter, chiles and garlic and spread on untoasted side. Combine mayonnaise and cheese. Place a generous amount of this mixture on top. Broil until brown and bubbly. These can be made ahead, refrigerated and broiled later.

Hot Wings

This recipe won't win over fans of traditional hot wings, but it is less troublesome to make and lower in fat.

⅓   cup yellow cornmeal
⅓   cup all-purpose flour
1   tablespoon ground cumin, from toasted seeds
1½ teaspoons salt
1½ teaspoons freshly ground black pepper
¾   teaspoon cayenne pepper
15 chicken wings (about 2½ pounds total)

Preheat oven to 375°F. Lightly brush a 12 x 17-inch jelly roll pan with oil, or spray with cooking spray.

Combine the cornmeal, flour, cumin, salt, and peppers. Separate the wings into segments. Reserve the tips for another use. Turn the wing segments in the cornmeal mixture, coating evenly. Shake off excess and arrange wings, without crowding, in the oiled pan.

Set the pan on rack in upper third of oven and bake, turning once at the halfway point, for about 60 minutes, or until crisp and evenly brown. Drain on paper towels and serve hot with sour cream and salsa. Makes 6–8 servings.

Thai Skewered Chicken

Lemon grass grows so well in this area and can be harvested and frozen for wintertime use. This is an appetizer I like to serve around holiday time.

1   cup minced lemon grass
2   tablespoons olive oil
2   tablespoons honey
1   onion, thinly sliced
2   jalapeno peppers, seeded and sliced
2   cloves garlic, minced
8   skinless, boneless chicken breast halves
1   red pepper, cored, seeded and julienned
8   scallions, green part only

Combine the lemon grass, olive oil, honey, onion, jalapenos and garlic in a large bowl. Add the chicken, turning to coat. Cover and refrigerate for 24 hours.

Preheat oven to 450°F. Remove a chicken breast from the marinade and with a sharp knife, butterfly it by making a horizontal cut into one of the long sides of the breast, and cutting to within ½ inch of the opposite side, keeping the top and bottom layers even in thickness. Place several strips of red pepper and a scallion at one short end of the chicken breast and roll up. Place seam-side down in a baking dish. Repeat with the remaining chicken breasts, red peppers and scallions.

Bake the chicken rolls for 5 minutes, until cooked through. Remove from the oven and allow to cool. Slice the chicken rolls crosswise into ½-inch pieces and place on a bamboo skewer. Makes about 48 appetizers.

Avocado Shrimp Tostados

These are time-consuming to assemble, but they're so tasty that it is worth it.
It is possible to put the avocado mixture and the shrimp in separate bowls
surrounded by a tray of chips, but I like the taste of all three together.

2	tablespoons lime juice
1	clove garlic, crushed
¼	cup vegetable oil
1	tablespoon minced cilantro
1	teaspoon dry mustard
¼	teaspoon ground cumin
½	teaspoon salt
¼	teaspoon freshly ground black pepper
12	medium shrimp, cooked and peeled
2	serrano chiles, seeded and minced
3	cilantro sprigs, minced
¼	cup minced onion
2	tomatoes, diced
2	avocados, coarsely mashed
24	round tostado chips
	Salt to taste
	Sour cream

Mix lime juice, garlic, vegetable oil, cilantro, mustard, cumin, salt, and pepper in
a bowl. Set aside. Devein the shrimp, split in half lengthwise, and toss with the
marinade. Refrigerate until ready to use. In a bowl, mix the chiles, remaining
cilantro, onion, tomatoes, avocados, and salt. Cover tightly until ready to use.

To serve, top each tostado chip with 1 teaspoon avocado mixture, a dollop of
sour cream and 1 shrimp. Garnish with a sprig of cilantro, if desired. Makes 24
appetizers.

Cheesy Chile Cups

Wonton skins are not just for wontons as they make nice carriers for appetizers. This filling is Tex-Mex, but you can fill them with sautéed mushrooms, Italian sausage, or pizza ingredients.

24   wonton skins cut into 3-inch rounds
1   cup shredded cheddar cheese
⅓   cup ricotta cheese
¼   cup canned green chiles, drained and finely chopped
1   tablespoon chopped chives or scallions
¼   teaspoon ground cumin
48   black olive slices

Preheat oven to 350°F. Spray two sets of miniature muffin tins with cooking spray. Place one wonton circle in each muffin cup, molding it to the cup, and lightly spray wontons with cooking spray. Bake in oven 7–8 minutes or until golden. Remove from tins and place on cookie sheets.

In a medium bowl, combine cheeses, chiles, chives and cumin. Mix well. Fill each wonton cup with 2 teaspoons of filling. Top with two olive slices. Bake 10 minutes or until bubbly. Serve warm. Makes 24 appetizers.

Chile Bacon Breadsticks

We make these and freeze them after they are cooked. They need only a quick defrosting before serving.

30 thin slices bacon (about 1 pound)
30 whole grissini (Italian breadsticks)
⅓ cup firmly packed brown sugar
3 tablespoons pure chile powder (preferably New Mexican)

Preheat oven to 350°F. Let bacon stand at room temperature to soften slightly, about 10 minutes. Wrap one bacon slice gently in a spiral around each breadstick and arrange on a tray.

In a shallow dish long enough to fit breadsticks, stir together brown sugar and chile, mashing out any lumps with the back of a fork. (Sugar mixture can also be forced through a sieve into a bowl.) Roll each breadstick gently in mixture, coating bacon well, and arrange about ½-inch apart on rack of a broiler pan.

Bake breadsticks 20 minutes or until coating is caramelized and bacon is deep golden brown. Loosen breadsticks gently from rack with a spatula and cool until firm enough to pick up, 10–15 minutes. Serve at room temperature. Makes 30 appetizers.

Herb-Roasted Mushrooms

These mushrooms are addictive — so make lots. They also make nice garnishes for meats and can be added to pasta or salads.

Juice of 1 lemon
2   teaspoons herbes de Provence
1   teaspoon hot pepper sauce
½   teaspoon salt
½   teaspoon freshly ground black pepper
½   cup olive oil
3   pounds large mushrooms, stems discarded, cleaned

Preheat oven to 450°F. In a medium bowl, combine the lemon juice with the herbes de Provence, hot pepper sauce, salt, and pepper. Stir in the olive oil. Add the mushrooms and toss until coated.

Spread the mushroom caps on a large non-stick baking sheet, stem sides up. Bake for 30 minutes. Turn mushrooms over and continue baking for about 15 minutes longer or until tender. Let cool completely before serving. Mushrooms can be refrigerated about five days. Makes about 30 mushrooms.

Scallop and Pesto Purses

Two purses on a small plate with a drizzle of basil oil make an elegant first course for dinner parties.

4   sheets phyllo dough
⅓   cup clarified unsalted butter
⅓   cup freshly grated Parmesan cheese
12   sea scallops
2   scallions, thinly sliced
3   tablespoons pesto

Center a rack in the oven and preheat oven to 375°F. Line a jelly roll pan with parchment paper and keep it close at hand. Cut 12 pieces of string into 6-inch lengths and butter the string.

Stack the sheets of phyllo on a work surface. Working with one sheet of phyllo at a time and keeping the others covered with a kitchen towel, brush a sheet with butter and sprinkle it with Parmesan cheese. Cover with a second sheet of phyllo and give it a coating of butter and a sprinkling of cheese. Using a long, sharp knife and a ruler as a guide, cut the sheets into rectangles by cutting lengthwise in half and then each half crosswise into thirds.

Place 1 scallop in the center of each of the 6 rectangles, top with a little sliced scallion, and add a dab of pesto. Gather up the corners of the rectangles, tie the purses with the buttered strings, and place them on the jelly roll pan. Repeat with the remaining phyllo and scallops. Bake the purses for about 12 minutes, or until golden brown. Snip off the strings and serve immediately. Makes 12 servings.

Puff Pastry Cheese Sticks

Keeping a package of frozen puff pastry in your freezer enables you to make these quickly for unexpected guests. Remember that puff pastry needs to be cold when it goes into a hot oven.

1   egg yolk
1   tablespoon milk
1   package frozen puff pastry sheets (2 sheets)
    Freshly grated Parmesan cheese or finely shredded Swiss cheese

Preheat oven to 400°F. Lightly beat the egg yolk with the milk to make a glaze.

On a lightly floured surface, unfold 1 sheet of pastry. Brush with egg-milk glaze; sprinkle with cheese. Press cheese gently with rolling pin. Turn sheet over and repeat.

Cut sheet in half crosswise; then cut into 5 x ½-inch strips. Twist each strip into a spiral by twisting ends in opposite directions. Place strips 1 inch apart on ungreased baking sheets. Repeat with remaining pastry. Bake 12–15 minutes or until puffed and golden brown. Remove from sheets and cool on racks. Makes 80 sticks.

Hot Mushroom Spread

I sometimes put this mixture into toast cups for an hors d'oeuvre that is passed. The cups can be filled and then popped into an oven for reheating.

4	slices bacon, cooked and crumbled
8	ounces fresh mushrooms, cleaned and chopped
1	onion, finely chopped
1	clove garlic, minced
2	tablespoons flour
	Freshly ground black pepper to taste
1	(8-ounce) package cream cheese, cubed
2	teaspoons Worcestershire sauce
1	teaspoon light soy sauce
½	cup sour cream
1	teaspoon lemon juice
¼	cup chopped nuts for garnish
½	loaf each cocktail rye and pumpernickel breads
	Paprika

Sauté mushrooms, onion and garlic in a small amount of bacon drippings. Whisk in flour. Add pepper, cream cheese, Worcestershire sauce, and soy sauce. Cook until cheese is melted. Blend in sour cream, lemon juice, and bacon, and warm slowly until heated through. Do not boil. Sprinkle with paprika and chopped nuts. Serve warm with breads.

Scallops Ceviche

In ceviche, the seafood cooks in the lime juice marinade. This recipe can be an appetizer with tostado rounds as scoopers or as a first course served in seafood shells.

1	pound fresh bay scallops
1	cup fresh lime juice, or enough to cover scallops
2	cloves garlic, very finely chopped
1	red bell pepper, seeded, ribs removed, finely diced
2	green chiles, seeded and finely diced
½	bunch cilantro, stems removed, coarsely chopped
1	large tomato, peeled, cored, squeezed, finely diced
½	cup olive oil

Slice scallops in thirds, cutting to preserve shape. Place in a bowl, add lime juice, and let marinate for 1 hour. Add garlic, peppers, cilantro, tomato, and olive oil. Mix well. Serve immediately or within 2–3 hours. Makes 4 servings.

Shrimp Dip

Shrimp is a party favorite and this recipe gives you the flavor without the cost of serving individual shrimp.

¼ cup packed fresh flat-leafed parsley leaves
½ medium onion
2 scallions
¾ pound shrimp, cleaned, deveined, and cooked
4 ounces cream cheese, softened
⅓ cup sour cream
¼ cup mayonnaise
1½ tablespoons bottled chile sauce or cocktail sauce
1 tablespoon fresh lemon juice
1½ teaspoons drained bottled horseradish
1 teaspoon Worcestershire sauce
½ teaspoon minced garlic
¾ teaspoon lemon pepper or lemon dill seasoning
2 dashes hot sauce
Thin, crunchy breads such as bagel chips, toast rounds or pita chips

Finely chop parsley and onion. Thinly slice scallions and coarsely chop shrimp. In a medium bowl, stir together cream cheese, sour cream, and mayonnaise until smooth. Stir in parsley, onion, scallions, shrimp, and remaining ingredients until combined well and season with salt and pepper. The dip keeps, covered and chilled, 1 day. Makes 3½ cups.

Smoked Salmon Cheesecake

Good smoked salmon is wonderful just by itself, but sometimes you need to extend it to make more servings. This smoked salmon has the creamy, rich texture of a dessert cheesecake.

1	tablespoon butter
3	tablespoons dry breadcrumbs
2	tablespoons freshly grated Parmesan cheese
14	ounces cream cheese (about 1 ¾ cup)
2	eggs
3	tablespoons heavy cream
½	cup chopped leeks, white part only
3	tablespoons unsalted butter
4	ounces smoked salmon, cut into small pieces
2	tablespoons grated Parmesan cheese
¼	cup grated Gruyere cheese
½	teaspoon white pepper
½	teaspoon salt

Butter a 12 x 3 x 4-inch loaf pan. Preheat oven to 300°F. Mix the crumbs and cheese and sprinkle on the pan until the sides and bottom are well covered. Turn the pan upside down over the sink and tap to shake out excess crumbs.

Let cream cheese soften to room temperature. Place the cream cheese, eggs, and cream in food processor bowl and process until smooth and fluffy; set aside. Sauté the leeks in butter until soft and translucent, about 5 minutes. Fold the leeks into the cheese mixture along with the diced smoked salmon. Add the Parmesan, Gruyere, and pepper. Add salt to taste.

Pour the cheese mixture into the loaf pan and place in a shallow baking pan. Add hot water to come half-way up the sides of the loaf pan. Bake the loaf for 1 hour and 40 minutes, turn off the oven, and let it sit in the oven for an additional hour. Remove it from the oven and let it sit at room temperature for at least 2 hours before unmolding. You may prepare it a day in advance and reheat it in a preheated 300°F oven for 20 minutes or until warm but not hot, then unmold. Makes 6 appetizer or 4 entrée servings.

Camembert Mousse

This creamy cheese spread is the ultimate cheese ball.

1   (8-ounce) wheel of Camembert
1   cup unsalted butter
6   tablespoons dry vermouth
3   to 4 dashes of hot sauce
    Toasted almonds, finely chopped

Trim rind from cheese (freezing the cheese for 10–15 minutes makes this easier). Cut cheese into small cubes and process with butter in food processor until well mixed. Gradually add vermouth and Tabasco until consistency of thick mayonnaise. Shape in center of plate and refrigerate. When firm, cover mousse with almonds, pressing them in. Serve with dry toast or water crackers. Makes about 1 pound.

Mushroom Piroshki

These freeze very well either baked or unbaked. If making not too far in advance, I completely bake, cool, and freeze them so they just require reheating before serving.

DOUGH:

1	cup unsalted butter
1	(8-ounce) package cream cheese
½	teaspoon salt
2	cups all-purpose flour
1	egg yolk
2	teaspoons milk

MUSHROOM FILLING:

8	ounces fresh mushrooms
2	tablespoons unsalted butter
½	cup chopped onion
½	teaspoon salt
	Freshly ground black pepper to taste
	Dash of freshly grated nutmeg
1	teaspoon fresh lemon juice
2	teaspoons all-purpose flour
½	cup sour cream
1	teaspoon dried dill

FOR THE DOUGH: Beat butter, cheese, and salt together until smooth. Work in flour. Flatten dough to form an 8 x 6-inch rectangle. Chill overnight. Remove from refrigerator about 15 minutes before using. (Divide dough for ease in handling and keep unused portion in refrigerator. Roll on floured pastry cloth or floured flat surface with a rolling pin and sleeve.)

Divide pastry in half and roll each half in rectangle ⅛-inch thick. Fold it over itself in thirds, roll again, fold it over in thirds again and roll in 10-inch square. Cut in 2½-inch rounds. Stack trimmings in layers; reroll. Put a level teaspoon of filling in center of each round; moisten edges with water and fold together over filling. Lay on sides and press edges with floured fork tines. Set pastries seam side up on ungreased cookie sheet. Chill 1 hour. Lightly beat egg yolk and milk to make a glaze; brush chilled pastries with glaze and bake in preheated 350°F oven for 25–30 minutes or until golden.

FOR THE FILLING: Trim and clean mushrooms. Chop until fine. Heat butter in a heavy skillet. Add mushrooms and onions. Sauté for about 5 minutes. Sprinkle salt, pepper, nutmeg, lemon juice and flour on top. Cook 2 minutes longer. Remove from heat; blend in sour cream and dill. Cool before filling pastry. Makes about 48.

Parmesan Cookies

Don't be tempted to use anything other than the real Parmesan here since it is the only ingredient. These cookies can also be made free form and served with soups and salads as a garnish.

12   ounces Parmegiano-Reggiano cheese, grated

Preheat oven to 350°F. Place a 3-inch ring mold or round cookie cutter on a large non-stick baking sheet and sprinkle about 2 tablespoons of the cheese into the mold in an even layer. Repeat to make more cookies. Bake for 9–10 minutes, until golden brown. Immediately remove each cookie with a spatula and place it over a rolling pin, so it makes a curved shape. They will crisp as they cool. Repeat until all the cheese is used. Makes 24 cookies.

Goat Cheese with Salsa

When we were just a two-person store, this was a lunchtime favorite.

1   log of goat cheese
    Picante salsa
    Tortilla chips
    Chopped fresh cilantro

Preheat oven to 375°F. Place goat cheese log on oven-proof plate. Mash to form an even layer. Place in oven until just melted and beginning to bubble. Remove from oven. Cool slightly before topping with salsa and cilantro. Serve with tortilla chips.

Pesto Pinwheels

This filling can also be used to make yeast bread pinwheels with bread dough from your bread machine. Having puff pastry rolls in your freezer means you can have an appetizer ready to bake with just a quick defrosting.

1   (8-ounce) package cream cheese, softened
1   cup grated Parmesan cheese
3   scallions, sliced (both green and white parts)
⅓   cup basil pesto
16 ounces frozen puff pastry, thawed, but cold enough to roll
1   cup black olives, chopped and blotted dry

Preheat oven to 350°F. Combine cream cheese, Parmesan cheese, scallions, and pesto; mix well. On a lightly floured surface, roll out each puff pastry sheet into a 10 x 16-inch rectangle.

Evenly spread cream cheese mixture over pastry sheets, completely covering them. Sprinkle half the olives on each sheet. Roll up each sheet like a jelly roll. Freeze rolls at least 3 hours or up to 2 months.

When ready to bake, remove rolls from freezer and let thaw 15–20 minutes, then slice into ¼-inch rounds. Put rounds on lightly greased baking sheet. Bake 10–12 minutes, or until lightly browned. Serve warm. Makes about 100.

Smoked Trout Mousse
with Horseradish and Dill

I sometimes divide this recipe into two small loaf pans and serve them with crackers or dry toast rounds when I need an appetizer for a small gathering. Making two means that I can save one if not needed, or bring a fresh one to the table during the party.

	Vegetable oil
1	tablespoon powdered gelatin
¼	cup cold water
2	smoked trout, total weight about 1½ pounds, skin and bones removed, flesh flaked with a fork
2	eggs, hard-cooked and coarsely chopped
3	scallions, trimmed, finely sliced with trimmed green tops
1	small bunch of fresh dill, stripped from stems and finely chopped
½	cup mayonnaise
½	cup plain yogurt or sour cream
3	tablespoons horseradish, more to taste
	Juice of 1 lemon
	Salt and freshly ground white pepper to taste
¾	cup heavy cream
1	bunch of watercress

Brush oil in interior of a 1½-quart terrine with lid. Sprinkle the gelatin over the cold water in a small bowl and let stand until granules become spongy, about 5 minutes. Mix the flaked trout, coarsely chopped eggs, scallions, dill, and mayonnaise in a medium bowl. Pour in the yogurt or sour cream. Add the horseradish, lemon juice, salt, and pepper and stir to blend the ingredients. Taste the mixture for seasonings.

Whip the cream in a chilled bowl until soft peaks form and set aside. Melt the gelatin in a small saucepan over low heat. Add it to the trout mixture and mix thoroughly. At once, fold in the whipped cream. Spoon the fish mixture into the oiled mold and smooth the top. Cover the mold with its lid and chill in the refrigerator until set, 3–4 hours. Run a knife around the edges of the mold. Dip the base of the mold in a bowl of warm water for a few seconds to loosen the mousse, then wipe the base of the mold dry. Set a platter on top of the mold and invert so that the mousse falls onto the platter. Cut the mousse into ¾-inch slices and set a slice on each plate and garnish with 1–2 sprigs of watercress. Makes 8–10 servings.

BLT Spread

Try this spread between two slices of grilled, buttered wheat bread. Add a bowl of soup for an easy lunch or light dinner. Use as a spread on dry bread rounds or mini toast cups.

8   slices bacon, fried crisp, drained and crumbled
1   medium tomato, finely chopped
½   small onion, finely chopped
¾   cup shredded Swiss cheese (about 3 ounces)
½   cup mayonnaise
1   teaspoon dried basil

Preheat oven to 375°F. Mix bacon, tomato, onion, cheese, mayonnaise and basil. Fill or spread and bake 5–10 minutes or until cheese is melted. Serve warm. Makes 24.

Cheese and Tomato Galette

½   recipe Galette Dough, chilled (recipe following)
2   ounces Monterey Jack cheese, shredded
2   ounces mozzarella, shredded
¼   cup fresh basil leaves, coarsely chopped or torn
2   to 3 firm but ripe plum tomatoes, cut into ¼-inch slices

Position a rack in the lower third of the oven and preheat the oven to 400°F. Line a baking sheet with parchment paper. Turn the dough onto a lightly floured work surface and roll it into an 11-inch circle that is about ⅛-inch thick. Toss flour under and over the top as you work to keep dough from sticking. Roll dough up around your rolling pin and unroll onto the prepared baking sheet.

Toss the cheeses and basil together. Sprinkle them over the rolled-out dough, leaving a 2–3-inch border. Place the tomatoes in concentric circles, one slice slightly overlapping the last, on top of the cheese. Fold the uncovered border of dough up over the filling, allowing the dough to pleat as you lift it up and work your way around the galette. Bake the galette for 35–40 minutes, or until pastry is golden and crisp and the cheese is bubbly.

Transfer the baking sheet to a cooling rack and let the galette rest on the sheet for 10 minutes. Slip a wide spatula or a small rimless baking sheet under the galette and slide it onto the cooling rack. Serve warm or at room temperature, garnished with fresh basil leaves. The galette can be kept at room temperature for several hours, but it is best served the day it is made. Makes 2–4 servings.

Galette Dough

3   tablespoons sour cream, yogurt or buttermilk
⅓   cup ice water
1   cup all-purpose flour
¼   cup yellow cornmeal
1   teaspoon sugar
½   teaspoon salt
7   tablespoons cold unsalted butter, cut into 5 to 8 pieces

Stir the sour cream and ⅓ cup ice water together in a small bowl; set aside. Put the flour, cornmeal, sugar, and salt in a work bowl of food processor with metal blade; pulse to combine. Add the butter in pieces to the bowl and pulse 8–10 times, or until the mixture is speckled with pieces of butter that vary in size from bread crumbs to peas. With the machine running, add the sour cream mixture and process just until the dough forms soft, moist curds.

Remove dough from the processor, divide in half, and press each half into a disc. Wrap in plastic and chill for at least 2 hours. Dough can be kept in the refrigerator for two days. It can be wrapped well and frozen for a month. Enough dough for two 8-inch rounds.

Hummus

Pita chips or dry toast rounds are good scoopers for this addictive dip.

1   (15-ounce) can chickpeas
2   cloves garlic
⅓   cup hot water
    Juice of 1 large lemon
¼   cup tahini
    Olive oil to taste
    Salt to taste
    Cayenne pepper to taste
    Ground cumin to taste

Drain and rinse the chickpeas with cold water. Process garlic in bowl of food processor with metal blade. Add chickpeas and process, gradually adding hot water to make a light, spreadable consistency. Add the lemon juice, tahini, olive oil, and seasonings to taste. Makes about 1 cup.

Chile Shrimp with Basil

In our catering we served a lot of shrimp with the classic red sauce, so when we are asked for something different I like to suggest these spicy shrimp. I use short bamboo skewers so they will be easy to eat.

2	tablespoons fish sauce
2	tablespoons lime juice
2	tablespoons water
2	teaspoons sugar
1	teaspoon Chinese chile sauce
2	cloves garlic, finely minced
2	tablespoons chopped fresh basil or ½ teaspoon dried
1	pound shrimp, cleaned, cooked and chilled
½	red bell pepper, finely diced
8	chives, snipped
2	tablespoons unsalted roasted peanuts, chopped

Combine the first seven ingredients and mix well.

About 30 minutes before serving, toss the shrimp with the sauce. Sprinkle the shrimp with the red bell pepper, chives, and peanuts. Serve at once. Makes 4 servings.

Pâte à Choux

These miniature puff shells are handy to have already baked for stuffing. I like to use a filling like Chutney Chicken Salad (see page 65).

1	cup cold water
	Pinch of salt
	Pinch of freshly ground white pepper
	Pinch of freshly ground nutmeg
6	tablespoons unsalted butter
1	cup all-purpose flour
4	eggs

Preheat oven to 375°F. In a saucepan, heat the water, salt, pepper, nutmeg, and butter to the boiling point. Remove from the heat. Add the flour all at once, stirring with a wooden spoon until the mixture forms a ball. Return the pan to low heat just until the mixture is warm. Add the eggs, one at a time, beating each thoroughly into the mixture. Using a pastry tube with a plain tip, make 1-inch puffs on an oiled baking sheet. Bake for 25 minutes until they are puffed and brown.

Turn off the oven and remove the pastries just long enough to make a small slit from top to bottom in the side of each. Return them to the turned off but warm oven; and with the oven door ajar, dry out the pastries for about 10 minutes. They should be hollow and dry on the inside.

Soups

The ultimate comfort food, soups know no season — any time of the year is soup time for me! Whether it is a light broth served as a first course or a hearty clean-out-the-refrigerator stew, soup makes a satisfying lunch or dinner. At our take-out counter, we sell almost as much soup during the summer months as during the winter.

And contrary to the idea that soups need to cook all day, many can be done in less than thirty minutes. Plus, many soups can be made in large quantities and frozen — a boon to busy cooks.

Hot and Sour Soup

The challenge in making this soup is getting the correct balance of hot and sour flavors. Ingredients vary, so taste often.

1	egg
2	tablespoons cornstarch
4	tablespoons water
6	ounces lean pork, cut into matchsticks
4	cups chicken broth
4	Chinese mushrooms, soaked, stems removed, cut into strips
1	slice gingerroot, peeled and minced
	Dried chile flakes to taste
2	cakes fresh tofu, cut into matchsticks
¾	cup bamboo shoots, cut into matchsticks
4	tablespoons cider vinegar
1	tablespoon light soy sauce
¼	teaspoon salt
¼	teaspoon freshly ground black pepper
½	teaspoon oriental sesame oil
6	scallions, finely chopped, green part included

Break egg into bowl and beat lightly. Mix cornstarch with water until well blended; set aside. Sauté pork until there is no pink. Drain fat. Bring broth to boil, add pork, mushrooms, minced gingerroot and chile flakes and bring to boil again. Reduce heat and simmer for about 10 minutes. Add tofu and bamboo shoots. Simmer for another 5 minutes. Mix vinegar, soy sauce, salt and pepper, and stir into soup. Add cornstarch mixture, stirring constantly until thickened. Stir in beaten egg and remove from heat when egg threads are firm. Add oil and decorate with scallions. Serve immediately. Makes 6–8 servings.

Tomato, Sausage, and Eggplant Soup

Even though the eggplant is beautifully shaped and colored, it is not a favorite vegetable of very many people. I think this soup uses its flavors well and makes a nutritious and hearty main course.

⅓ cup plus 2 tablespoons olive oil	4 bay leaves
4½ cups eggplant, peeled and cut in ½-inch cubes	1 teaspoon dried basil
1½ teaspoons salt	1¼ teaspoons dried thyme
1½ cups chopped onions	1 pound sweet Italian sausage with casing removed
½ cup chopped fennel or celery	1½ cups chicken stock
2 tablespoons minced garlic	1 (29-ounce) can heavy tomato puree
2 teaspoons ground or crushed fennel seed	1 (28-ounce) can whole peeled tomatoes, chopped
½ teaspoon freshly ground black pepper	

Heat ⅓ cup olive oil in 5-quart saucepan. Add eggplant and ½ teaspoon salt. Saute over medium-high heat, stirring frequently, for 4–5 minutes or until just tender. Transfer the eggplant to a bowl. In the same pan, heat the remaining 2 tablespoons of olive oil. Add the onions, fennel or celery, garlic, fennel seed, pepper, bay leaves, the remaining teaspoon of salt, basil and thyme. Cook over medium-high heat, stirring frequently, for 5–6 minutes. Add the sausage and saute 5–6 minutes, breaking up the meat into small pieces with a spoon. Add the stock, tomato puree, chopped tomatoes with their juice, and the eggplant. Cover and simmer 10–15 minutes. If the soup seems too thick, add more stock. Remove bay leaves before serving. Makes 3 quarts.

Chile Con Queso Soup

This soup is my son's favorite, and he doesn't object to using broken tortilla chips instead of frying tortillas.

½   large onion, finely chopped
2   cloves garlic, minced
3   tablespoons unsalted butter
1½ (4-ounce) cans mild green chiles, drained, seeded and finely chopped
2   (14.5-ounce) cans plum tomatoes, drained and finely chopped
6   ounces cream cheese, cut into bits
12   ounces cooked chicken breasts, finely chopped
2   cups chicken broth
1½ cups half-and-half
4   teaspoons fresh lemon juice (or to taste)
¼   teaspoon cayenne
½   teaspoon cumin
     Salt to taste
     Julienned tortilla strips, fried crisp
6   green onions, sliced into rings
1   cup grated Monterey Jack cheese

Cook onion and garlic in butter in a saucepan over moderately low heat, stirring occasionally, until onion is softened. Add chiles and tomatoes. Cook mixture 8–10 minutes over moderate heat until liquid evaporates, stirring occasionally. Stir in cream cheese. Maintain moderate to low heat until cheese melts. Stir in chicken, chicken broth, half-and-half, lemon juice and seasonings to taste. Heat soup over moderate heat until hot, but do not boil. Sprinkle tortilla strips, green onions and cheese over individual servings. Makes 12 cups.

Cream of Wild Mushroom Soup with Couscous

This is an elegant soup for a first course. I usually use a mix of dried and fresh mushrooms since a variety of fresh mushrooms is hard to find.

1	tablespoon extra-virgin olive oil
1	cup leeks, finely diced
1	cup onions, finely diced
1	tablespoon fresh garlic, chopped
1	teaspoon fresh gingerroot, minced
8	ounces mixed wild mushrooms, chopped (crimini, shiitake, oyster)
2	tablespoons light soy sauce
4	cups chicken stock
1	cup port wine
½	cup cream or half-and-half
3	tablespoons cornstarch mixed with 3 tablespoons water
	Salt and freshly ground black pepper to taste
2	cups cooked couscous

In a large soup pot, heat the olive oil and when hot, add the leeks and onions. When onions are golden brown, add the garlic and ginger root. When garlic is fragrant, add the mushrooms and soy sauce. Sweat them for 2 minutes; then add the stock and port. Bring to a boil and simmer for 25 minutes. Pour in the cream and cornstarch mixture and heat for only 2–3 minutes; do not boil. Adjust the seasonings. In each soup plate, place ¼ cup cooked couscous. Pour about 1 cup of soup in the plate. Makes 4–6 servings.

Couscous

⅔ cup water
1   tablespoon extra-virgin olive oil
    Salt to taste
½   cup couscous

In a saucepan, bring the water, oil and salt to a rolling boil. Add the couscous and immediately take it off the heat. Stir, cover and let sit for 5 minutes. Fluff it with a fork and serve.

Butternut Squash and Bourbon Bisque

This is a beautiful fall soup with the warm color of autumn. The contrast of the gingerroot and maple syrup flavors gives the soup added depth.

4   pounds butternut squash
1   tablespoon extra-virgin olive oil
1   cup onions, diced
1   cup leeks, diced
½   teaspoon ground cumin
2   tablespoons chopped fresh garlic
1   tablespoon chopped fresh gingerroot
2   tablespoons pure maple syrup
2   tablespoons light soy sauce
¼   cup bourbon
½   cup dry sherry
¼   teaspoon grated nutmeg
5   cups chicken stock
¾   cup milk, half-and-half, cream, or evaporated skim milk
     Salt and freshly ground black pepper to taste
2   tablespoons cornstarch mixed with 2 tablespoons water
     Croutons and sour cream for garnish

Preheat oven to 375°F. Prick the squash in several places to allow steam to escape while it cooks. Place the squash in a baking dish lined with foil and roast for about 90 minutes or until the squash is soft when you push on it. Let cool for 30 minutes. Peel, seed, and remove strings. Cut the roasted squash into ½-inch pieces. In a heavy soup pot, heat the olive oil and add the onions. Cook until light golden brown and add the leeks and cumin. Cook for 2 minutes and add the garlic and gingerroot. When the garlic is fragrant, add the maple syrup, soy sauce, bourbon, sherry and nutmeg. Add the squash and stock and bring to a boil. Lower the heat and cook gently for 15 minutes. Puree soup in a blender or food processor until very smooth. Add the milk, salt and pepper to taste. Return to stove, cook for 2 minutes; do not boil. Add the cornstarch mixture and cook until slightly thickened. Serve in soup plates. Garnish with croutons and sour cream. Makes 6 servings.

Hearty Minestrone

I like this minestrone because it combines beans, pasta and vegetables for a hearty bowl of soup. The last minute addition of spinach gives it a bright color contrast.

1   tablespoon extra-virgin olive oil
1   cup onions, chopped
1   cup leeks, chopped (white part only)
5   cups chicken stock
1½   cups potatoes, diced
1   cup orzo
1¾   pounds ripe tomatoes, peeled, seeded, and chopped (about 2 cups)
1   cup white beans, cooked al dente
1   cup yellow squash, chopped
1   cup zucchini, chopped
2   cups spinach leaves, stemmed
     Salt and freshly ground black pepper to taste
¼   cup freshly grated Parmesan cheese

In a soup pot, heat the olive oil and then add the onions. Sauté for 2 minutes and then add the leeks. Cook for 3 minutes. Add the stock and potatoes. Bring to a boil and reduce heat immediately to a slow simmer. Cook for 5 minutes. Add the orzo and cook for 5 additional minutes. Add the tomatoes, beans, squash and zucchini. Cover and cook until vegetables are tender. Stir in the spinach and cook for 3 minutes. Adjust seasonings. To serve, ladle into bowls and sprinkle with Parmesan cheese. Makes 6 servings.

Tiffanys' Bean Pot Soup

Tiffanys' was a restaurant I visited in Cerrillos, New Mexico, many years ago. I was fascinated by this "clean out the spice cabinet" soup which freezes beautifully.

2	cups dry pinto beans	1	bay leaf
1	pound ham, cubed	1	teaspoon oregano
4	cups water	½	teaspoon ground cumin
2	(13.5-ounce) cans tomato juice	½	teaspoon rosemary leaves
4	cups chicken stock	½	teaspoon celery seeds
1	medium onion, chopped	½	teaspoon thyme
3	cloves garlic, minced	½	teaspoon ground marjoram
3	tablespoons parsley, chopped	½	teaspoon basil
¼	cup green bell pepper, chopped	¼	teaspoon curry powder
4	tablespoons brown sugar	4	whole cloves
1	tablespoon chile powder	1	cup dry sherry
1	teaspoon salt		

Thoroughly wash and soak beans overnight; drain. Add remaining ingredients except the sherry. Bring to boil, reduce heat and simmer, covered, until beans are tender. Add sherry; reheat to serving temperature. Makes about 3 quarts of soup which can be divided and frozen.

Puree of Pumpkin Soup

Fresh is better, but the sugar pumpkin requires peeling and cleaning. I don't think you'll notice that much difference between the canned and fresh in this soup.

4	tablespoons unsalted butter
1	large onion, chopped
1	medium size leek, white part only, chopped
1	pound of pumpkin puree, fresh or canned
4	cups chicken stock
1	teaspoon salt
½	teaspoon curry powder
¼	teaspoon ground nutmeg
¼	teaspoon freshly ground black pepper
¼	teaspoon ground ginger
1	bay leaf
1	cup half-and-half

Melt butter and sauté onion and leek. Stir in pumpkin, stock and seasonings. Bring to a boil. Lower heat and simmer, uncovered, for 15 minutes, stirring occasionally. Remove the bay leaf. Puree the mixture in batches in a food processor or a blender. Return to pot. Add half-and-half and cook over moderate heat, stirring occasionally, until heated through. Adjust the seasonings to taste. Makes 6–8 servings.

Vegetarian Chili

You won't miss the meat in this hearty chili. It is a favorite from our take-out counter.

8 ounces dry red kidney beans, washed, drained, and soaked overnight
1 teaspoon salt
1 (14-ounce) can Italian tomatoes
½ cup raw bulgur
2 cloves garlic, peeled
1 small onion, peeled and quartered
1 celery rib, cut into 1-inch pieces
1 medium carrot, peeled and cut into 1-inch pieces
1 small green bell pepper, cored, seeds and ribs removed
2 tablespoons vegetable oil
2 tablespoons chopped parsley
2 tablespoons dry red wine
1 tablespoon tomato paste
1 tablespoon fresh lemon juice
1 teaspoon chili powder
½ teaspoon ground cumin
3 drops hot sauce
   Freshly ground black pepper to taste
½ cup shredded Cheddar cheese

Put the beans in a saucepan with 4 cups of water and bring to a boil. Reduce heat to low, cover and cook until tender, about 1 hour. Salt to taste. Strain liquid from tomatoes into a small saucepan, reserving tomatoes. Bring liquid to boil, add bulgur, cover and remove from heat. Set aside for at least 15 minutes.

Insert metal blade in bowl of food processor and turn on the machine. Drop the garlic through the feed tube and process until minced. Add the onion and pulse until coarsely chopped. Set aside. Still using the metal blade, process the celery, carrot and pepper, pulsing until coarsely chopped. Set aside. Puree tomatoes with metal blade, processing about 15 seconds.

Heat oil in a large skillet over moderate heat. Add garlic and onion and cook, stirring, until onion is tender, about 3 minutes. Add chopped vegetables, pureed tomatoes, 1 tablespoon chopped parsley, and remaining ingredients except cheese. Cook 5 minutes longer, stirring often, or until vegetables are barely tender. Stir vegetable mixture and bulgur into undrained kidney beans; reheat if necessary. Sprinkle cheese and remaining parsley over top and serve. Makes about 4–6 servings.

Spicy Corn Chowder

Soup making can be done quickly with a few convenience foods. I probably wouldn't serve these convenience foods by themselves, but I am grateful for the time saved when I use them such as in this recipe.

6   slices bacon, cut into julienne strips
½   cup onion, chopped
¼   pound small mushrooms, cleaned and sliced thin
1½ cups raw potato, diced
½   cup water
1   (17-ounce) can cream-style corn
1   (10.5-ounce) can condensed cream of mushroom soup
2   cups milk
1   teaspoon salt
1   (4-ounce) can green chiles, seeded and chopped

Cook bacon until crisp; drain and reserve. Pour bacon fat from pan, leaving 3 tablespoons in pan. Stir-fry onion, mushrooms and potato in reserved bacon fat, about 5 minutes or until golden. Stir in water, cover and simmer for 15 minutes or until potato is tender. Add corn, soup, milk and salt and bring just to boiling; stir in chiles. Lower heat and let simmer about 5 minutes. Ladle into soup bowls and top each portion with reserved bacon. Makes 6 servings.

Tomato Pesto Soup

Tomatoes and pesto are unbeatable together. Summer is the best time for this soup.

2   tablespoons shallots, chopped
5   cups tomatoes, peeled, seeded, and diced
1   tablespoon olive oil
1   tablespoon garlic, chopped
1   cup tomato juice
¼   cup pesto
      Salt and freshly ground black pepper to taste
1   cup heavy cream
      Sour cream and chopped fresh basil for garnish

Sauté the shallots and tomatoes in the olive oil. Add the garlic and tomato juice and cook for about 20 minutes. Let the mixture cool, puree and then pass it through a fine sieve. Return the soup to the pan, place over medium heat, and add the pesto. Season to taste and stir in the cream.

To serve this soup hot, bring to just below a boil. If you prefer it cold, refrigerate the soup after adding the cream. Garnish each serving with a dollop of the sour cream and a sprinkling of the basil. Makes 6–8 servings.

Pesto

2   cups fresh basil leaves, washed, dried and with stems removed
2   tablespoons pine nuts or walnuts, toasted
4   medium garlic cloves
⅓   cup olive oil
½   cup Parmesan cheese, freshly grated

In a food processor with the metal blade, combine all the ingredients except the cheese. Process until smooth, stopping several times to scrape down the sides of the bowl. Transfer the mixture to a bowl and stir in the cheese.

Cream of Carrot Soup

This soup requires few ingredients, so it is easy to have when I am craving comforting soup. Sometimes I add lemon and dill seasonings. Other times I might add ginger or curry flavorings. You can also reduce the fat by using evaporated skim milk or low-fat milk instead of cream for the enrichment.

2	tablespoons butter
5	to 6 medium carrots, chopped
1	medium onion, chopped
	Pinch of sugar
	Salt and freshly ground black pepper to taste
4	to 5 cups chicken stock
½	cup uncooked rice
2	tablespoons butter
¾	cup heavy cream

Melt the 2 tablespoons butter in a heavy-bottomed pot. Add the carrots, onion, sugar, salt and pepper. Cover and cook over low heat for 5–7 minutes or until butter is absorbed and the vegetables are very soft. Add 4 cups of stock and the rice. Bring to a boil, cover, reduce heat and simmer 25–30 minutes until the rice and carrots are very tender. Puree the soup in the food processor or blender. Return the soup to the pan and bring just to a boil, adding more stock if necessary to make the consistency of thin cream. Add the cream, bring just back to a boil and taste for seasoning. Take off the heat and stir in the butter until just melted. Serve with croutons. Makes 6 servings.

White Chili

This recipe looks formidable because of its length, but it actually goes together very quickly. The complexity of the different layers of flavors makes it very tasty. If you can't find all the peppers and pure ground chile, use all jalapenos and chili powder mix.

1	pound Great Northern or navy beans	1	tablespoon cumin seed, toasted and crushed
8	cups water	1¼	pounds skinless, boneless chicken breasts
½	cup onion, chopped		
2	cloves garlic, minced	1	(14.5-ounce) can chicken broth
1	teaspoon salt	2	tablespoons ground New Mexico chile
	Freshly ground black pepper		
12	ounces Mexican beer (not dark)	1	pound tomatillos, husks removed
2	cups onions, diced	1	cup minced fresh cilantro
1½	tablespoons garlic, minced	1	tablespoon rice vinegar
1	cup diced red bell pepper,	1	teaspoon salt
2	jalapeno chiles, seeded and diced	2	cups grated sharp white cheddar cheese
4	Anaheim or New Mexico green chiles, roasted, peeled and seeded		Cilantro leaves for garnish
1	tablespoon dried oregano		

Pick over beans for debris. Place in a colander and rinse well. Place in large pot with water, onion, garlic cloves and a grating of fresh black pepper. Simmer for 2–3 hours, until the beans are tender. Add salt during last 30 minutes of cooking.

While beans are cooking, place the beer in a 4-quart pot. Add the onions, garlic, bell pepper, jalapenos, green chiles, oregano and cumin. Simmer for 10 minutes. Cut the chicken into strips, then dice. Add to the pot along with the chicken broth. Sprinkle in the ground chile and simmer for 15 minutes.

Place the tomatillos, minced cilantro, vinegar and salt in a food processor and process to a salsa consistency. Stir into the chili. Add the drained cooked beans and simmer for 20 minutes. Taste for seasoning. Ladle into serving bowls. Sprinkle ⅓ cup of the cheese over each serving and broil until the cheese is golden. Garnish with cilantro. Makes 6 servings.

Gazpacho

When I first got my food processor, I looked forward to making this soup in it. Part of the enjoyment of this soup for me is the beautiful diced vegetables floating in the juice so I have returned to doing this soup by hand.

1	cup peeled tomatoes, finely chopped	1	small clove garlic, minced
¼	cup onion, finely chopped	2	to 3 tablespoons tarragon wine vinegar
½	cup finely chopped green bell pepper	2	tablespoons olive oil
½	cup celery, finely chopped	1	teaspoon salt
½	cup finely chopped cucumber	½	teaspoon freshly ground black pepper
2	teaspoons chopped parsley	½	teaspoon Worcestershire sauce
½	teaspoon chives or scallions, snipped	2	cups good quality tomato juice

Combine all ingredients in a glass bowl or pitcher. Cover and chill for 4–6 hours. For a spicier soup, add Tabasco, salsa and or chopped jalapenos to taste. Makes 6 servings.

Black Bean Chili

You will notice the fragrance of the cumin and oregano when you toast them. A little heat awakens these spices and makes them more pungent.

4	cups black beans	1½	tablespoons paprika
2	large yellow onions, finely chopped	1	teaspoon salt
		3	cups canned tomatoes, crushed
1½	cups finely chopped green bell peppers	½	cup finely chopped jalapeno chiles
2	cloves garlic, minced	½	pound Monterey Jack or Cheddar cheese, grated
½	cup olive oil	⅔	cup sour cream
2	tablespoons cumin seed	½	cup scallions, finely chopped
2	tablespoons oregano		Chopped cilantro
1	teaspoon cayenne pepper		

Sort and rinse beans. Cover with cold water and soak overnight. Rinse beans and put them into a large pot with water several inches above the top of beans. Cover and bring to a boil. Reduce heat and cook until tender. Add more water if needed. When beans are cooked, strain and reserve 1 cup of bean liquid and add it back to the beans.

Toast cumin seed and oregano until fragrant, either on the stove or in 325°F oven for 10 minutes. Sauté onions, green peppers and garlic in oil with cumin seed and oregano, cayenne pepper, paprika and salt for 10 minutes or until onions are soft. Add tomatoes and chiles. Add all to the beans, stir and reheat. To serve, place 1 ounce grated cheese, then 1¼ cups hot chili in a heated bowl. Top with a spoonful of sour cream and sprinkle with 1 tablespoon scallions and some cilantro. Makes 8 generous servings.

Salads

Remember when just a wedge of iceberg lettuce was considered a salad?

Today, salad greens can be purchased in a bag, already cleaned and ready to dress. The choice of greens can range from ordinary iceberg to the more exotic raddichio. Dressings can be hot or cold, creamy, or just vinegar and oil. Classic crouton toppings share honors with toasted goat cheese, sautéed mushrooms, and even grilled meats. In fact, salads are not just side courses anymore — they often are the main course itself.

Included in this section are salad recipes that I've had for over twenty years, as well as some that are much more contemporary.

Le St. Germain Mushroom Salad

Le St. Germain in Los Angeles was my introduction to a real French restaurant. Their magnificent floral arrangements were matched by the quality of the food they served.

½   teaspoon salt
½   teaspoon freshly ground black pepper
1   tablespoon Dijon mustard
2   tablespoons red wine vinegar
3   tablespoons dry red wine
½   cup plus 2 tablespoons peanut oil
1½   pounds mushrooms, cleaned and sliced
    Fresh parsley, minced

Combine all ingredients except mushrooms, parsley and oil. Slowly beat in oil so that the dressing emulsifies. Toss with sliced mushrooms and minced parsley before serving. Makes about 8 servings.

Chinese Shredded Chicken Salad

Although this recipe is called Chinese, I got it from a Japanese cousin of my best friend. Twenty years ago the ingredients were hard to find in Columbus, and the recipe was considered rather exotic. It is still delicious because the flavors are delicate and light.

2   tablespoons sugar
1   teaspoon salt
½   teaspoon freshly ground black pepper
3   tablespoons vegetable oil
2   tablespoons oriental sesame oil
2   tablespoons cider vinegar

4   to 8 ounces rice noodles
4   chicken breasts cooked, skin removed, meat shredded
1   head of iceberg lettuce
4   scallions, sliced diagonally, green part included
2   tablespoons sesame seeds, toasted

Combine first 6 ingredients and shake well until sugar is dissolved. Taste and adjust vinegar and sesame oil to taste.

Break noodles into manageable handfuls and fry in hot oil until puffed. Drain on paper towels. (Noodles can be fried a day ahead and stored in an air-tight container.) Shred lettuce (this also can be done several hours ahead if lettuce is washed and dried well before cutting).

To serve, toss lettuce, chicken, and scallions with well shaken dressing. Add noodles and toss once more. Sprinkle sesame seeds on top and serve immediately. Makes 6–8 servings.

Spinach and Apple Salad

I am sure we prepare more spinach salads now because of the availability of bagged baby spinach. Whatever the case, I'm glad to be able to have this salad whenever I want.

⅔   cup corn oil
¼   cup red wine vinegar
2   tablespoons light soy sauce
1   teaspoon dry mustard
1   teaspoon sugar
½   teaspoon salt
2   teaspoons fresh lemon juice
2   dashes hot sauce
     Freshly ground black pepper to taste
1   pound fresh spinach, trimmed, washed and dried
3   small Jonathan or Granny Smith apples, cored and coarsely chopped
¼   cup toasted sunflower seeds

Whisk together all ingredients except spinach, apples and sunflower seeds. Toss spinach and apples with enough dressing to coat well. Add sunflower seeds. Makes 6 servings.

Paella Salad

This salad has many of the characteristics of a classic paella but can be served without last minute preparation.

1 ¼ cups olive oil
2   cups raw long-grain rice
5   cups chicken stock
2   generous pinches of saffron
1½ teaspoons salt
⅓   cup red wine vinegar
1½ pounds large shrimp, cooked and shelled with tails left on, deveined
½   cup red bell pepper, julienned
½   cup green bell pepper, julienned
1   cup green peas, cooked and drained, or defrosted if using frozen
½   cup black olives, cut into quarters
¼   cup chopped fresh parsley
¼   cup chopped fresh chives
     Several large leaves Boston lettuce, rinsed and dried

In a large casserole with a lid, heat ¼ cup of the oil over medium-high heat. When the oil is hot, add the rice and cook, stirring until rice is opaque, about 2–3 minutes. Add the stock, saffron and ½ teaspoon salt. Stir well to dissolve the saffron. Bring mixture to a simmer. Lower the heat and cook, covered, until all the liquid has been absorbed, about 20 minutes. When the rice is cooked, remove the lid and let it cool to room temperature. Assemble salad by placing the vinegar and the remaining 1 teaspoon salt in a large bowl. Whisk in the remaining 1 cup of olive oil. Add the shrimp, red and green peppers, peas and olives. Let marinate 10 minutes. Add the rice, parsley and chives. Mix well. To serve, arrange a border of lettuce leaves on a large serving platter and place rice mixture in the center. Serve at room temperature. Makes 6 servings.

Lentil Salad with Goat Cheese

French green lentils keep their shape after cooking so they are preferred for salads.

1½ tablespoons sherry wine vinegar
1 tablespoon Dijon mustard
¼ teaspoon ground cumin
¼ teaspoon sugar
Salt and freshly ground black pepper to taste
5 tablespoons olive oil
1 cup French green lentils, cooked until just tender, drained
1 medium red onion
½ yellow or green bell pepper
½ red bell pepper
1 small jalapeno pepper
¼ cup fresh cilantro or mint leaves
4 ounces soft goat cheese

Combine vinegar, mustard, cumin, sugar, salt and pepper in a small dish and stir until sugar dissolves. Add the olive oil and mix well. Add the mixture to the warm lentils and let stand until cooled to room temperature.

Meanwhile, dice the onion and peppers. Remove seeds and ribs from the jalapeno and mince. Mince the cilantro or mint. When lentils are cooled, add vegetables, jalapeno and cilantro or mint. Mix gently. Crumble the goat cheese into the salad and mix lightly so the cheese stays in pieces. Serve immediately or refrigerate overnight. Adjust seasonings before serving. Makes 4 servings.

Greek Salad

The Greek olives and cheese give this salad its distinctive flavors. Don't be tempted to substitute these two important flavor ingredients.

1	large head romaine lettuce
2	heads red leaf lettuce
2	bunches watercress
2	cucumbers, peeled, seeded and coarsely chopped
16	radishes, thinly sliced
8	large scallions including some green, chopped
2	(15-ounce) cans garbanzo beans, drained and rinsed with cold water
24	Kalamata olives, pitted and halved
1	pound feta cheese, cut into ½-inch cubes
1	small can anchovy fillets, drained, dried and finely chopped, optional
6	tomatoes, cut in wedges
	Salt and freshly ground black pepper to taste
1	cup olive oil
⅔	cup red wine vinegar
3	cloves garlic, minced
1½	teaspoons dried oregano, crumbled
⅓	cup chopped fresh parsley

Wash greens, break off stems and tear leaves into bite-size pieces. Wrap in paper towel and place in plastic bag; refrigerate overnight to crisp. In a medium bowl, gently toss cucumbers, radishes, scallions, garbanzo beans, olives, feta cheese and anchovies. Combine dressing ingredients. Pour over vegetables and marinate, covered, in the refrigerator for 4–12 hours. At serving time, pour vegetables with their dressing over greens and toss. Add tomatoes and season to taste. Makes 16 servings.

Strawberry Chicken Salad

Strawberries and chicken make an unlikely combination, but surprisingly enough they taste great together.

¼	cup mayonnaise
½	cup sour cream
1	medium shallot, minced
2	tablespoons capers
1	tablespoon caper juice
½	teaspoon salt
¾	teaspoon white pepper
4	whole chicken breasts, cooked, skin removed, meat shredded
1½	cups sliced strawberries
3	tablespoons slivered almonds, toasted
	Lettuce leaves for garnish

Combine mayonnaise, sour cream, shallot, capers, caper juice, salt, and pepper. Refrigerate for 1 hour so flavors can blend. Toss chicken with sour cream mixture. Add strawberries gently, being careful not to bruise them. Refrigerate for 30 minutes or until thoroughly chilled. Spoon onto lettuce-lined plates. Add almonds to top. Salad may also be served on halved avocado, papaya or pineapple. Makes 6 servings.

Smoked Chicken, Pear, and Walnut Salad with Gorgonzola

Sometimes I make this salad without the chicken when I want to serve it with dinner. It is interesting to add dried cranberries or cherries and to change the combination of greens. Don't be afraid to experiment.

⅓ cup walnut halves
2 tablespoons balsamic vinegar
1 tablespoon fresh lemon juice
1 tablespoon Dijon mustard
¼ teaspoon minced garlic
  Salt and freshly ground black pepper to taste
6 tablespoons walnut oil
1 head Belgian endive
½ small head raddichio
1 cup loosely packed watercress, large stems removed
1 head butter lettuce
1 ripe Bosc, Bartlett, or Comice pear
1 cup skinned and smoked chicken breast, julienned (about 6 ounces)
⅓ cup crumbled Gorgonzola or other similar blue cheese

Preheat oven to 375°F. Place walnut halves on a baking sheet and bake until they appear toasted, about 5 minutes. Remove from oven, cool and coarsely chop. Reserve. Whisk together the balsamic vinegar, lemon juice, mustard and garlic. Whisk in the walnut oil. Season to taste and set aside. Slice the endive in half lengthwise. Remove the base. Cut the halves crosswise into ½-inch pieces. Place in a salad bowl. Remove the core from the raddichio half and cut the leaves into bite-size strips; add to the bowl with the endive. Wash and dry the watercress. Add to the bowl. Remove the core from the butter lettuce. Tear the leaves into small pieces. Wash and dry. Add to the bowl. Cut the pear in half lengthwise.

Remove its core and any fibers coming down from the stem. Slice the halves thinly and add to the bowl. Add the chopped walnuts and the julienned smoked chicken to the bowl. Add the vinaigrette and toss well. Sprinkle the crumbled blue cheese on top and serve at once. Makes 2 entrée servings.

Beef Tenderloin Salad with Chile, Red Onion, and Cucumber

Fish sauce is to Thai cooking what oyster sauce is to Chinese. It plays a similar role as Worcestershire sauce.

½ pound beef tenderloin
2 tablespoons water
2 tablespoons lime juice
2 tablespoons fish sauce
1 teaspoon red chile flakes
1 medium cucumber, thinly sliced crosswise
1 large red onion, thinly sliced
¼ cup scallions, cut on the diagonal into 1-inch lengths
¼ cup chopped cilantro leaves
¼ cup mint leaves
6 lettuce leaves for serving

Grill meat to medium rare and set aside. In a saucepan, combine water, lime juice, fish sauce, and chile flakes and bring to boil. Simmer for one minute. Slice meat, add to the liquid in the pan and allow it to absorb some of the sauce. Place mixture into large bowl and add the cucumber, red onion, scallions, cilantro and mint. Gently mix the ingredients until all are coated with the sauce. Place mixture inside lettuce leaves to serve. It may also be served on a plate with bite-sized chopped lettuce to one side. Makes 4 first course servings.

Julienned Vegetable Salad

Home cooks can quickly produce beautiful salads like this with a mandoline.

1	small carrot, peeled
1	stalk celery, tough strings removed
1	small red bell pepper, seeded and membranes removed
1	small yellow bell pepper, seeded and membranes removed
1	fennel bulb (bulb part only)
1	small zucchini
1	small yellow squash
½	cup jicama
1	cup peanut oil
½	cup olive oil
½	cup white wine vinegar
2	tablespoons balsamic vinegar
2	shallots, finely chopped
2	cloves garlic, finely minced
2	teaspoons each finely chopped fresh basil, parsley, chives, tarragon, and thyme
	Salt and freshly ground black pepper to taste
	Juice of ½ lemon or to taste

Cut all vegetables into matchstick-size julienne. Combine all vegetables in a large bowl. In a medium bowl, combine remaining ingredients and season to taste. Pour over julienned vegetables. Marinate for 10 minutes or up to several hours. Serve at room temperature, tossing well before serving. Makes 6 servings.

Twenty-four-Hour Salad

*This is the gourmet version of the classic overnight salad. You will like the
addition of spinach, red pepper, and herbs to the old favorite recipe.*

1	pound spinach, stemmed, rinsed, dried and torn into bite-size pieces
1	red bell pepper, cut into 1½ x ¼-inch strips
3	scallions, cut into ½-inch lengths
1	large head of romaine lettuce, rinsed, dried and torn into bite-size pieces
½	red onion, very thinly sliced
½	pound Swiss cheese, shredded
1	(10-ounce) package frozen peas
4	hard-cooked eggs, sliced
1⅓	cups sour cream
⅔	cup mayonnaise
½	cup chopped parsley
⅓	cup minced fresh chives
2	cloves garlic, minced
1	tablespoon fresh lemon juice
1	tablespoon red wine vinegar
2	teaspoons Dijon mustard
½	teaspoon salt
¼	teaspoon freshly ground black pepper
1	pound sliced bacon, cooked until crisp and crumbled

Layer the first 8 ingredients in a large bowl in the order listed. In another bowl,
combine the sour cream, mayonnaise, parsley, chives, garlic, lemon juice, vinegar,
mustard, salt and pepper. Whisk to blend well. Spread the dressing over the top
of the salad to cover it completely. Cover the bowl with plastic wrap and
refrigerate up to 24 hours. Shortly before serving, toss the salad. Save about ½
cup of the bacon and add the rest to the salad. Toss salad again. Sprinkle the
reserved bacon on top. Makes 12 servings.

Salads

Salad Miramonte

The nutty taste of the Gruyere cheese combines nicely with the bacon in this salad.

¾   cup vegetable oil
3   tablespoons fresh lemon juice
2   cloves garlic, minced
     Salt and freshly ground black pepper to taste

1   to 2 heads romaine lettuce, cleaned, dried and torn into bite-size pieces
4   slices bacon, fried crisp, drained and crumbled
10   ripe cherry tomatoes, stemmed and halved
1   cup grated Gruyere cheese
⅓   cup grated Parmesan cheese

⅔   cup toasted slivered almonds
1   cup French bread croutons

Combine first four ingredients to make dressing. Allow flavors to blend. Shake well and toss with lettuce, bacon, tomatoes, and cheeses just before serving. Add almonds and croutons and toss again. Makes 4–6 servings.

Orange and Spinach Salad with Honey-Mustard Dressing

If fresh oranges are not in season, you can subsitute a can of drained mandarin orange slices.

¾ cup vegetable oil
¼ cup red wine vinegar
¼ cup honey
¼ cup Dijon mustard
¼ cup sesame seeds, toasted
2 cloves garlic, minced
½ teaspoon freshly ground black pepper
½ teaspoon salt
1¼ pounds fresh spinach, stems removed, washed and dried
2 large oranges, peeled and sectioned
1 small red onion, thinly sliced
½ pound bacon, cooked, drained and crumbled

Combine dressing ingredients and mix well. Tear spinach into bite-size pieces. Add oranges and onion. Toss salad with just enough dressing to coat. Sprinkle top with bacon. Makes 6 servings.

Cobb Salad

This salad was very popular when I lived in Los Angeles because it originated at the Brown Derby Restaurant, a place where movie stars liked to be seen. I am reminded of it now when I see so many chopped salads on restaurant menus.

½	head firm iceberg lettuce		Extra-virgin olive oil
1	bunch watercress		Salt and freshly ground black
1	small head of chicory		pepper to taste
½	head romaine	¼	cup water
2	whole poached chicken breasts	¼	cup red wine vinegar
	(see following)	¼	teaspoon sugar
2	tablespoons minced chives	1½	teaspoons lemon juice
2	medium tomatoes	½	teaspoon salt
6	strips bacon, cooked until crisp,	½	teaspoon freshly ground black
	drained		pepper
3	hard-cooked eggs	½	teaspoon Worcestershire sauce
1	ripe, firm avocado	¾	teaspoon Dijon mustard
2	ounces Roquefort cheese or best	1	clove garlic, minced
	quality blue cheese	¼	cup extra-virgin olive oil
1	lemon	¾	cup vegetable oil

Clean and spin dry the salad greens. Remove any parts that are not tender. Use only the leaves of watercress. Refrigerate in plastic bag to crisp greens. Cut the chicken into a fine dice. Toss chicken in a small bowl with salt and pepper and a few drops of olive oil. Cover and refrigerate. Mince bacon and set aside. Chop or sieve eggs, mix in chives, sprinkle with salt and pepper, and set aside. Dice cheese and set aside. Peel, seed and juice the tomatoes. Dice and set aside. Halve the avocado, peel and dice. Toss with a bit of olive oil and lemon juice.

To make the dressing combine water, vinegar, sugar, lemon juice, salt, pepper, Worcestershire sauce, mustard, garlic and oils. Shake dressing well before using. Makes about 1½ cups.

When ready to serve, toss the mixed greens and arrange in the bottom of a wide bowl. Arrange in rows the different ingredients on top of the greens. Recombine the dressing and add to the salad just before serving.

Poached Chicken Breasts

2   whole chicken breasts, boneless and skinless
½   cup dry white wine or dry vermouth
1   bay leaf
1   shallot
3   parsley sprigs
4   peppercorns
½   teaspoon salt

Lay chicken breasts in a lightly buttered saucepan just large enough to hold them in one layer. Pour in wine and enough water to cover the breasts. Add remaining ingredients and bring to a simmer, cover and cook at a very low simmer for 8–10 minutes, until the meat is done (do not overcook; it should be springy to the touch). Let cool for 30 minutes in the broth. Remove breasts, let cool, wrap in plastic wrap, and refrigerate. (The broth can be saved and added to soup, if desired.)

Shrimp and Capers in Tomato Mayonnaise

This recipe is at its best when made with homemade mayonnaise, but to avoid the raw eggs I use a good brand of prepared mayonnaise and flavor it with Dijon mustard and lemon juice.

1	pound uncooked medium shrimp, cleaned and deveined
2	tablespoons vegetable oil
½	cup loosely packed parsley leaves
1	medium shallot, peeled
1	medium tomato, peeled and seeded
¼	teaspoon sugar
1	teaspoon dried basil
2	tablespoons capers, rinsed and patted dry
½	teaspoon salt
	Freshly ground black pepper to taste
1	cup mayonnaise

Wash shrimp quickly in water and pat dry. Sauté in oil over medium heat until just cooked. Drain thoroughly and let cool. Mince parsley in food processor with metal blade. Set aside. Mince shallot and set aside. Coarsely chop tomato and place into mixing bowl. Add sugar, basil, capers, salt, pepper, mayonnaise, and shallot. Combine well. Mix with well-drained shrimp. Adjust salt and pepper to taste. Marinate for 2 hours. Drain off liquid if necessary and add more mayonnaise just before serving. Serve on lettuce leaves. Sprinkle with minced parsley. Makes 4–6 servings.

Mayonnaise

1 whole egg
1 tablespoon fresh lemon juice or white wine vinegar
1 tablespoon Dijon mustard
Salt
1 ¼ cups light olive or vegetable oil, or a mixture of both

Process egg, juice or vinegar, mustard, salt and 1 tablespoon of oil in food processor with metal blade. Pour ¼ cup of oil very slowly through the feed tube with the machine running. When it has emulsified, gradually add remaining oil. Taste and adjust the seasonings. Cover and refrigerate. Makes 1½ cups.

Chutney Chicken Salad

Curry is a blend of spices and can vary from brand to brand. I prefer Madras Curry Powder, but domestic brands will do.

5 cups cooked chicken breasts, cut into bite-size pieces
3 hard-cooked eggs, chopped
1 (8-ounce) can water chestnuts, drained and chopped
¼ cup scallions (white and some of the green) diced
1 cup celery, diced
1 cup green bell pepper, diced
1¼ cups mayonnaise
¼ cup mango chutney
2 tablespoons white wine vinegar
2 teaspoons curry powder
3 tablespoons sour cream
Salt to taste

Combine mayonnaise, chutney, vinegar, curry, sour cream and salt. Pour over other ingredients and toss. Makes 10 servings.

Red Cabbage and Bacon Salad with Blue Cheese

Blanching the cabbage and tossing it with vinegar sets the color to a beautiful pink/red. The tart dressing, bacon and cheese make this salad a winner.

½   head red cabbage (about 1½ pounds)
¼   cup red wine vinegar
2   quarts boiling water
1   small head romaine lettuce
3   ounces blue cheese
½   pound thick-cut bacon
¼   cup red wine vinegar (or more, if needed)
1   tablespoon Dijon mustard
¾   cup olive oil
    Salt and freshly ground black pepper to taste

Combine vinegar with the mustard and a pinch of salt. Grind in pepper. Whisk in oil to emulsify. Taste for seasoning.

Set the cabbage half cut-side down on the chopping board. Trim the stem end and discard. Peel off any outside leaves that are wilted. Cut the cabbage lengthwise in half. Rest the stem end of 1 piece on the chopping board; cut out the core and discard. Repeat with the other piece. Finely shred the cabbage quarters. Discard any thick ribs. Transfer the shredded cabbage to a large bowl. Heat the vinegar to boiling in a small saucepan. Pour the vinegar over the shredded cabbage and toss to mix so it is thoroughly coated. Pour the boiling water over the cabbage and let stand until slightly softened, 3–4 minutes. Drain in a colander, then return it to the large bowl. Toss the cabbage with enough vinaigrette to moisten it well. Taste for seasoning, add more vinegar if necessary. Cover the bowl and marinate the cabbage in the dressing, 1–2 hours.

Twist off and discard the root end from the lettuce. Discard any wilted leaves. Wash the lettuce well under cold running water, then drain leaves thoroughly. Remove and discard thick stems. Stack the leaves and roll them up quite tightly, slice crosswise into wide strips. Crumble the blue cheese into a small bowl with your fingers, making sure that the pieces are not too small.

About ten minutes before serving, stack the bacon slices and cut crosswise into strips. Cook the bacon in the frying pan, stirring occasionally, until crisp and the fat is rendered, 3–5 minutes. Spoon the hot bacon and pan drippings over the red cabbage, reserving some bacon pieces for garnish. Toss them together. Arrange a bed of shredded lettuce leaves on 6 individual plates. Spoon any remaining dressing over the lettuce. Mound the red cabbage and bacon mixture in the center. Top salads with the blue cheese and reserved bacon. Serve at once. Makes 6 servings.

Asparagus and Pecan Salad

Damon Fowler, recognized authority on Southern cooking, has brought several delightful classes to our store. He served this salad as a prelude to his Creole Fried Chicken.

3   pounds asparagus
    Salt
½   cup freshly squeezed lemon juice
2   tablespoons Dijon mustard
¼   teaspoon sugar
2   tablespoons parsley, chopped
1   tablespoon fresh thyme or tarragon, chopped
1   cup extra-virgin olive oil
    Freshly ground black pepper
6   medium scallions, trimmed and thinly sliced
1   cup toasted pecans, chopped
2   large hard-cooked eggs, peeled and forced through a sieve

Fill a basin with cold water. Wash the asparagus, trim off the stem end, and peel the tough skin from the lower part of the stalk with a vegetable peeler. Drop each asparagus into cold water as it is trimmed. Soak the asparagus in the water at least 30 minutes before cooking.

Put about 1 inch of water into a large, shallow pan that will hold the asparagus in no more than 2 layers. Cover and bring to a boil over high heat. Add several large pinches of salt to the water, let it come back to a boil, then add the asparagus. Cover the pan until the water comes back to a boil, then uncover and cook until the asparagus is crisp-tender, about 3–4 minutes. Drain and refresh the asparagus under cold running water. Set aside.

In a glass or stainless steel bowl, combine the lemon juice, mustard, a pinch of salt and the sugar, and beat until the mixture is smooth. Add 1 tablespoon parsley and the thyme or tarragon and stir well. Whisking constantly, gradually add the oil a few drops at a time until it is all incorporated and emulsified. Taste and adjust the salt and sugar and add several liberal grindings of black pepper. The dressing should not be sweet. Beat until the seasonings are well mixed.

Spread the asparagus on a serving platter. Sprinkle the scallions and half the dressing over the asparagus and gently toss until it is lightly coated. Scatter the top with pecans, remaining parsley, and sieved eggs and serve at once, passing the remaining dressing separately. Makes 8 servings.

Roasted New Potato Salad

This potato salad is lighter and healthier than one made with mayonnaise. It tastes best if never refrigerated.

3	pounds small new potatoes
	Olive oil
	Salt and freshly ground black pepper to taste
1	tablespoon lemon juice
1	tablespoon Dijon mustard
2	cloves garlic, finely chopped
1	tablespoon chopped fresh thyme or 1 teaspoon dried thyme
5	tablespoons white wine vinegar
½	teaspoon salt
1	teaspoon freshly ground black pepper
1¼	cups extra-virgin olive oil
½	small white onion, thinly sliced
2	celery stalks, thinly sliced
8	scallions, including some of the green tops, finely chopped
2	tablespoons chopped fresh chives
1	tablespoon chopped parsley, flat-leaf preferred

Preheat oven to 400°F. Wash the potatoes and cut in half if any are larger than 1-inch. Lightly coat them with olive oil. Spread out on a bake sheet and generously sprinkle with salt and pepper. Bake for 30–35 minutes, turning several times. Potatoes should feel tender when pierced with the tip of a knife. Set aside to cool to room temperature.

Prepare the vinaigrette by whisking together the lemon juice, mustard, garlic, thyme, vinegar, salt and pepper. In a slow steady stream whisk in the olive oil until completely incorporated. Vinaigrette may be made 2 days ahead and refrigerated. Before using, bring to room temperature and shake.

In a large bowl toss together the potatoes and half of the vinaigrette. Reserve remainder for other use. Add the sliced onion, celery, and three-fourths of the scallions. Toss well. Set aside for 1–2 hours. When ready to serve, sprinkle with the remaining scallions, the chives and parsley. Makes 6 servings.

Mediterranean Couscous Salad

Couscous is great summer eating because although a pasta, it is not at all heavy or filling. It also lends itself to many flavor combinations.

1½	cups water
½	teaspoon salt
¼	teaspoon freshly ground black pepper
1	cup couscous
¾	cup crumbled feta cheese
1	large tomato, coarsely chopped
½	cup loosely packed shredded fresh basil leaves
⅓	cup scallions, thinly sliced
⅓	cup pitted Kalamata olives, coarsely chopped
⅓	cup olive oil
3	tablespoons lemon juice

In a 2-quart saucepan, bring water, salt and pepper to boil. Stir in couscous and cover pan. Remove from heat and let stand 5 minutes. Fluff couscous lightly with a fork. Cool to room temperature. In a large bowl, combine couscous, cheese, tomato, basil, scallions, olives, oil and lemon juice. Chill before serving. Makes 6 servings.

Thai Pasta Salad

This salad is great as a meatless side dish or you can add bits of cooked chicken, shrimp or pork to make it more substantial.

8	ounces linguine
⅓	cup scallions, sliced
½	cup carrots, finely julienned
1½	cups Napa cabbage, thinly sliced
1½	cups red cabbage, thinly sliced
1	cup bean sprouts
½	cup pea pods, julienned and blanched
1	tablespoon brown sugar
⅓	cup white wine vinegar
3	tablespoons peanut butter
1	teaspoon garlic, minced
1	teaspoon gingerroot, minced
½	teaspoon red pepper flakes
2	tablespoons vegetable oil
2	tablespoons water
1	tablespoon light soy sauce

Cook linguine in boiling, salted water. When al dente, drain and rinse with cold water. Add scallions, carrots and cabbages. Mix brown sugar, vinegar, peanut butter, garlic, gingerroot, red pepper flakes, vegetable oil, water and soy sauce. Combine dressing with pasta mixture. Cover and refrigerate until serving. Fold in sprouts and pea pods just before serving. Makes 8 servings.

Tabbouleh

When my son was a preschooler, I would get together with a cooking friend so our children could play. We would spend the morning preparing recipes together and then divide the results to take home to be enjoyed by our families. This was before the use of food processors, so the only way to have this recipe was to chop by hand. You can now use your chopping gadget of choice.

2	cups uncooked bulgur (cracked wheat)
1	cup loosely packed parsley leaves
1	cup loosely packed mint leaves
¾	cup scallions, sliced
4	cups seeded tomatoes, chopped
1	teaspoon salt
½	teaspoon freshly ground pepper
2	tablespoons olive oil
½	cup lemon juice

Place bulgur in a bowl and cover with water. Mix with fingers to wash and drain off water. Cover bulgur with 4 cups hot water and let soak at room temperature about 2 hours or until bulgur is al dente. Drain remaining water off bulgur and place bulgur in a clean dish cloth. Squeeze out excess water. Place bulgur in large mixing bowl. Wash and dry parsley and mint. Finely chop and add to bulgur along with the remaining ingredients. Toss until combined. Cover and refrigerate about 3 hours before serving. Makes 8 cups.

Breads

Nothing beats freshly baked bread straight from the oven or bread machine! Adding breads — whether yeast breads, cornbread, or biscuits — can turn even a simple meal into something special.

Pesto Biscuits

Freshly baked bread of any kind makes a meal special. This quick biscuit goes nicely with any type of Italian dish.

2	cloves garlic
2	cups all-purpose flour
2	teaspoons baking powder
½	teaspoon baking soda
¼	teaspoon salt
⅓	cup lightly packed basil leaves
⅓	cup shortening or butter
3	tablespoons grated Parmesan cheese
⅔	cup milk, regular, low fat or skim
2	tablespoons pine nuts, toasted
1	egg beaten with 1 teaspoon water

Place oven rack in upper third of oven and preheat oven to 425°F. In food processor with metal blade, process garlic until minced. Add flour, baking powder, baking soda, salt, and basil. Pulse until well combined and basil leaves are coarsely chopped. Add shortening or butter and 2 tablespoons of the Parmesan cheese. Pulse until mixture resembles coarse meal. Add milk and 1 tablespoon of the pine nuts and pulse just until dough comes together.

Turn dough onto a lightly floured board and knead gently about 6 times. On a lightly greased baking sheet or parchment paper, shape the dough into a 7-inch round, ½-inch thick. With a knife, cut dough round into 12 wedges, not quite through to the bottom. Brush top with egg and water mixture and sprinkle with the remaining 1 tablespoon of Parmesan and 1 tablespoon of pine nuts, pressing them into the dough. Bake 15–18 minutes or until golden brown. Serve warm, breaking or cutting along scoring. Makes 12 biscuits. (Note: Prepared pesto can be used instead of the garlic, basil, and cheese mixture in the batter.)

Pesto Roll

This yeast bread freezes well. I like to make baguette-sized loaves and freeze them baked but unsliced. Then when I need a loaf, I can just defrost, reheat and slice. Try it toasted with a slice of fontina or provolone melted on top.

1½	teaspoons dry yeast	8	ounces shredded mozzarella cheese
1½	teaspoons sugar	½	cup grated Parmesan cheese
1	cup warm water (105°F–110°F)	1	egg, lightly beaten
¼	cup olive oil	1	teaspoon coarsely ground black
1½	teaspoons salt		pepper
2½	cups unbleached flour	½	cup pesto

Combine yeast with the warm water and add sugar. When yeast is dissolved, add olive oil.

Combine salt and flour in food processor bowl with the metal blade. Pulse to mix. With machine running, slowly add yeast mixture through the feeder tube. Process until mixture forms a ball and is kneaded. Place dough into oiled bowl, cover, and let rise until doubled. Punch dough down and roll out to about a 26 x 18-inch rectangle.

Combine mozzarella, Parmesan, beaten egg, pepper, and pesto. Spread this mixture evenly over the surface of the dough. Starting with a long edge, roll dough into a long loaf and transfer to a lightly greased baking sheet. Tuck ends under and pinch all seams. Cover dough with a sheet of greased plastic wrap and let rise until doubled, about 60–90 minutes. Bake in preheated oven at 400°F for 40 minutes or until golden brown. Remove loaf from oven and transfer it from the pan to a rack. Let cool for 20 minutes before slicing.

Texas Cornbread

This meat and vegetable filled cornbread is more entrée than bread. I always like to include it on a Tex-Mex buffet table.

1	pound pork sausage	½	cup all-purpose flour
1	yellow onion, chopped	1	teaspoon baking soda
1	green bell pepper, seeded and chopped	1	teaspoon sugar
1	tablespoon butter	1	teaspoon baking powder
3	eggs	¾	cup milk
1	cup sour cream	6	ounces prepared salsa
¼	cup soft butter	8	ounces Monterey Jack or Longhorn Cheddar cheese, shredded
1	cup cooked corn kernels		
1¼	cups stone ground cornmeal		

Preheat oven to 350°F. In a skillet over medium heat, sauté the sausage until no longer pink. Drain, reserving 2 tablespoons of fat, and set aside. In the same skillet, sauté the onion and pepper in the reserved fat and 1 tablespoon of the butter until onions are translucent. Remove from heat.

Combine eggs, sour cream, butter and corn in bowl of food processor with the metal blade, and process until corn is minced. Stir together the dry ingredients and add to the workbowl. With machine running, pour the milk through the feeder tube; process just until ingredients are mixed.

Pour ⅔ of the batter into a buttered 9 x 13-inch rectangular dish or into two buttered 8-inch pie pans. Top the batter with a layer each of sausage, pepper and onion, salsa, and cheese in that order. Top with remaining ⅓ batter. Bake 40–45 minutes until just set and the cornbread has a consistency of a quiche. Let stand for 10 minutes before cutting into wedges or squares. Serve warm. (You may cut into large pieces for an entrée or into small squares for an appetizer.) Makes 8 servings.

Raspberry Almond French Toast

This is the all-time French toast favorite from our annual brunch class.

4	brioches or 16 small slices egg bread
1	cup frangipane (recipe follows)
½	cup good quality raspberry preserves
3	eggs
3	egg yolks
¾	cup milk
½	teaspoon almond extract
2	tablespoons unsalted butter
	Confectioners' sugar

Preheat oven to 350°F. If using brioches, slice each in 4 horizontal slices. Spread half of the slices of brioche or bread with a tablespoon of frangipane. Spread the remaining slices generously with raspberry preserves and put together with frangipane-coated slices, coated sides together, to make 8 sandwiches.

In a shallow baking dish, whisk together the eggs, egg yolk, milk and almond extract. Place the sandwiches in the mixture and let them soak about 20 minutes, turning occasionally.

Melt the butter over low heat in a large skillet. Sauté the sandwiches about 3 minutes per side and transfer to a baking dish. Bake about 10 minutes to melt the fillings. Dust with confectioners' sugar and serve immediately. Makes 4 servings.

Frangipane

1   cup blanched almonds
1   tablespoon all-purpose flour
8   tablespoons unsalted butter, room temperature
½   cup sugar
2   egg yolks
1½ teaspoons almond extract
    Pinch of salt

Combine the almonds and flour in food processor bowl and process until finely ground. Transfer to a bowl and reserve. Process the butter until smooth. Add the sugar, egg yolks, extract and salt. Process until fluffy. Add the ground almonds and combine by pulsing. Refrigerate until firm enough to spread, about 1 hour. Makes 1 cup.

Baked French Toast with Blueberries

This French toast recipe is probably the second favorite of the many prepared over the years for the annual brunch class.

1   to 1½ loaves of French bread, crust removed and sliced ¾-inch thick
8   eggs
1   cup milk
¾   teaspoon vanilla extract
½   cup butter, softened
1   cup brown sugar
¼   cup flour
1   cup rolled oats (not instant)
1   cup chopped walnuts
1   to 2 cups blueberries

Grease a 6 x 10-inch baking dish. Preheat oven to 375°F. Place bread slices in a single layer in the bottom of the prepared pan. Cut additional bread into small pieces to fill in spaces around slices. Beat eggs and milk together and add vanilla extract. Pour egg mixture over bread. (There should be enough liquid to cover bread. Add more milk if necessary.) Let the bread, egg, and milk mixture set one or two minutes to allow bread to absorb the egg mixture. Turn bread slices to evenly soak both sides.

With a pastry blender, blend together the butter, brown sugar, and flour. Stir in the oats. Spread walnuts and blueberries over the soaked bread in baking dish. Sprinkle oats mixture over all. Bake 30–40 minutes or until bread is puffy and bubbles rise around the sides of the pan. Let set 5 minutes before cutting into rectangles to serve. Makes 6–8 servings.

Cranberry Orange Scones

Dried cranberries and cherries are now available in most grocery stores, and add a lot of variety to our winter baking. You can use either in this recipe.

2   cups flour
1   tablespoon sugar
2   teaspoons baking powder
½   teaspoon salt
¼   cup butter
½   cup heavy cream
1   egg
1   cup dried cranberries
2   teaspoons orange zest

Preheat oven to 425°F. Combine dry ingredients in a large mixing bowl. Using a pastry blender, work butter into dry ingredients. Mix cream and egg and add to dry ingredients, mixing just until the dry ingredients are moistened. Add cranberries and orange zest.

Turn dough onto a lightly floured surface and gently knead into a ball. Pat into a circle ¾-inch thick and cut into 8 wedges, not quite through to the bottom. Place on lightly greased cookie sheet. Bake 12 minutes or until golden brown. Makes 8 scones.

Buttermilk Biscuits

If you haven't tried biscuit making using the time-saving food processor, don't wait another morning. Bake these on a hot pizza stone and see the biscuits rise almost immediately. The crusty exterior and soft insides literally melt in your mouth. Mary Lu Orr shared this recipe in a quick-bread class many years ago, and they are a regular Sunday morning treat at our house.

2	cups flour
1	tablespoon baking powder
¼	teaspoon baking soda
½	teaspoon salt
2	teaspoons sugar
½	cup unsalted butter
¾	to 1 cup cold buttermilk

Preheat oven with pizza stone to 450°F. In bowl of food processor with the metal blade, place the flour, baking powder, baking soda, salt, and sugar. Pulse to blend. Cut butter into eight pieces and add. Pulse until mixture resembles coarse meal. Add part of buttermilk and pulse until dough comes together, taking care to add only enough buttermilk to make a soft dough. Turn dough onto lightly floured surface and knead gently. Pat to ¾-inch thick and cut into rounds. Bake on hot baking stone 12–15 minutes at 450°F. Makes 12–16 biscuits, depending on the size of the cutter.

If a food processor is not available, in a large mixing bowl combine the dry ingredients. Cut in butter with a pastry blender until the mixture resembles coarse crumbs. Toss with just enough buttermilk to form dough. Pat out, cut, and bake as above.

Dill Bread in Clusters

The is a fun bread to make as you can be creative in how you arrange the bread clusters. Since we do a lot of wine tastings, this bread is perfect. Be imaginative.

½	cup warm milk	¼	cup minced fresh dill (or 2
3	tablespoons dry yeast		tablespoons dried)
4	teaspoons brown sugar	4	eggs
2	cups large-curd cottage cheese	1	tablespoon salt
4	tablespoons unsalted butter or	½	teaspoon baking soda
	shortening	5	cups all-purpose flour
		2	tablespoons milk

Whisk milk, yeast, and sugar in large bowl until blended. Let stand until foamy. Generously grease another large bowl. Mix cottage cheese, butter, dill, 2 eggs, salt and baking soda in food processor until smooth. Add to yeast mixture, blending well. Stir in 1 cup flour and mix thoroughly. Gradually add remaining flour, mixing just until dough comes away from sides of bowl. Turn dough out onto lightly floured board and knead until smooth and elastic. Place in greased bowl, turning to coat all surfaces. Cover and let rise until doubled, about 1¼ hours.

Preheat oven to 350°F. Generously grease 3 baking sheets. Punch dough down and turn out onto lightly floured surface and divide into 3 portions. Working quickly, break off small walnut-sized pieces of dough and shape into balls. Arrange side-by-side on baking sheet into shape resembling grape clusters, reserving some of the dough to form stems and leaves for decoration. Repeat with remaining portions. Beat remaining 2 eggs with milk and lightly brush mixture over top of clusters. Let rise for 20 minutes. Bake 5 minutes and then rebrush with egg mixture. Bake another 15 minutes, watching carefully and covering loosely with foil if browning too quickly. Remove from oven and transfer bread to wire racks to cool. Makes 3 clusters.

Lithuanian Bacon Buns

This savory bread adds a bit of variety to a muffin basket at breakfast. The rolls can be frozen after baking and reheated before serving. Instead of a baking sheet, I like to use a twelve-cup muffin tin. The rolls are all uniform in size this way.

1	teaspoon salt	¼	cup sour cream
3	cups bread flour	½	pound sliced bacon, cut into ½-inch pieces
1	tablespoon sugar		
2¼	teaspoons dry yeast	¾	cup chopped onion
1	cup milk	1	egg, beaten

In a large bowl, combine 1½ cups flour, sugar, yeast, and salt. Combine milk and sour cream in a saucepan and heat until warm (120 °F). Stir milk and sour cream into dry ingredients. Stir in remaining flour to make soft dough. Knead on lightly floured surface until smooth and elastic, about 6–8 minutes. Cover and let rest 10 minutes.

In skillet, fry bacon until crisp; drain on paper towels. Pour drippings from skillet. In the same pan, sauté onion 4–5 minutes or until tender. Remove from heat. Combine bacon and onion in pan, and set aside.

Divide dough into 12 equal pieces, and flatten each piece to a 3½-inch round. Place 1 rounded tablespoon bacon filling on center of each. Bring up edges of dough to enclose filling; pinch to seal. Place pinched sides down on greased large baking sheet, about 2 inches apart. (If using muffin tin, spray with non-stick cooking spray.) Cover buns and let rise in warm draft-free place until doubled in size, about 30 to 45 minutes. Brush beaten egg over top of buns. Bake in preheated oven at 350°F for 15–20 minutes or until golden brown. Remove from pan and cool on wire racks. Makes 12 buns.

Currant-Walnut Baguettes

This bread has just a hint of sweetness and is delicious with cheese at the end of a meal.

1	package dry yeast	¾	cup walnut halves
1½	tablespoons honey	¾	cup currants
1¼	cups warm water (105°F–110°F)	¼	cup golden raisins
1½	cups bread flour	¼	cup raisins
1½	cups whole wheat flour	1	egg, beaten
1	teaspoon salt		

Dissolve yeast and honey in ¼ cup warm water. With plastic dough blade in food processor bowl, combine flours and salt. Add walnuts and process 15 seconds. With machine running, pour the yeast mixture through the feeder tube. Process until dough clears the sides of the bowl and is no longer dry, about 1 minute more.

Turn dough out onto a lightly floured board and knead in the currants and raisins for about 5 minutes. Transfer dough to oiled or buttered bowl, turning to coat the top with the butter. Cover and let rise until doubled, about 2 hours.

Turn dough onto a lightly floured board. Punch down and divide in half. Roll each half into a 6 x 15-inch rectangle. Starting from the long edge, roll each rectangle into a long cylinder shape, pinching the edges to seal. Transfer the loaves, seam side down, to two greased baguette pans. Cover with plastic wrap that has been sprayed with non-stick cooking spray and let rise until almost doubled, about 45 minutes. Brush loaves with beaten egg and slash each loaf several times diagonally. Bake in preheated oven at 425°F for 30–40 minutes, until loaves are well browned. Makes 2 loaves.

beef ❧ poultry ❧ pasta ❧ fish ❧ pork

Entrées

beef ❧ poultry ❧ pasta ❧ fish ❧ pork

The main course of a meal used to be a piece of meat, but that has changed in recent years. Our well-traveled population thinks nothing of cooking ethnic dishes or serving vegetarian recipes as the main part of a meal.

The recipes from our twenty years of cooking classes contain traditional recipes such as pot roasts, as well as many ethnic and meatless dishes.

Chicken Chile

The buttermilk in this recipe tenderizes the chicken and the overnight marinating makes the recipe perfect for entertaining.

6	whole chicken breasts, boneless and skinless	1	large onion, finely chopped
3	eggs, lightly beaten	1	clove garlic, peeled, minced
1½	cups seasoned soft bread crumbs	⅔	cup canned green chiles, chopped
⅔	cup vegetable oil	1	(14-ounce) can Italian plum tomatoes, coarsely chopped
6	tablespoons butter	1	(8-ounce) package cream cheese
1	large green pepper, finely chopped	1½	to 2 cups buttermilk

Cut chicken breasts into halves and lightly pound to flatten. Dip chicken in beaten eggs, then dredge in bread crumbs, coating lightly but thoroughly. Set chicken pieces on rack to dry for 10–15 minutes.

Heat a skillet over medium heat and add oil and butter. When hot, lightly sauté chicken. Remove to rack to drain. Pour off excess oil and reheat pan over medium heat. Sauté pepper, onion, and garlic. Add chiles and tomatoes and stir over low heat. Cut cream cheese into small pieces and add to vegetable mixture; cook, stirring, until mixture is creamy.

Spread ⅓ of the vegetable-cream cheese sauce over the bottom of a 9 x 13-inch baking dish. Arrange chicken pieces on top of sauce, overlapping pieces if necessary. Cover chicken with remaining sauce. Pour buttermilk over the chicken, using only what is necessary to barely cover the chicken. Tip dish back and forth a bit to distribute the buttermilk. Cover with plastic wrap and refrigerate 8 hours or overnight. (The flavor improves if it is allowed to stand overnight.)

Allow the dish to come almost to room temperature, and bake in preheated oven at 350°F for 30 minutes. Add more buttermilk if the dish appears to be dry. Makes 12 servings.

Chinese Lemon Chicken

*What a surprise I had when I ordered Lemon Chicken on my trip to
China — it was so sweet and cloying compared to the lightness of this recipe!*

2	tablespoons light soy sauce	1	cup chicken broth
½	teaspoon sesame oil		Zest of 1 lemon, finely chopped
1	teaspoon salt		Juice of 1 lemon
1	tablespoon gin, vodka, or dry sherry	2	tablespoons lemon extract, or to taste
4	whole chicken breasts, boneless and skinless	3	egg whites
		¼	cup all-purpose flour
2	tablespoons cornstarch	¼	cup cornstarch
4	tablespoons water		Peanut oil
¾	cup sugar	½	head iceberg lettuce, thinly shredded
½	cup white vinegar		

Combine the soy sauce, sesame oil, salt and gin, vodka, or sherry in a large dish.
Add chicken breasts and turn to coat. Marinate chicken breasts, turning
occasionally, for at least 30 minutes.

Mix the 2 tablespoons cornstarch with the 4 tablespoons water until smooth.
Place in a saucepan. Add sugar, vinegar, broth, lemon zest, and lemon juice, and
blend well. Bring to a boil. Reduce heat and cook until sauce thickens. Keep hot.

Remove chicken from the marinade and drain; discard the marinade. Beat the
egg whites just until frothy. Combine flour and cornstarch and put mixture into a
flat plate. Dip the chicken pieces in the egg white, then coat lightly with the flour
and cornstarch mixture. Heat ½-inch of peanut oil in a skillet. When oil is hot,
add chicken, a few pieces at a time and cook until golden brown and done, about
8–10 minutes per side. Drain on paper towels.

Cut chicken pieces crosswise into 1-inch pieces. Arrange chicken on top of the shredded lettuce. Stir lemon extract into the hot sauce and spoon over the chicken pieces. Serve immediately. Makes 4–6 servings.

Roast Chicken with Rosemary, Sun-dried Tomatoes, and Lemon

Whether you eat the skin or not, leave it on the chicken because it naturally bastes the meat while cooking. The aroma of this dish while roasting fills the house and will remind you of traveling the Mediterranean.

1	whole chicken, 3½–4 pounds
1	lemon, cut into very thin slices and seeds removed
¼	cup rosemary leaves (or 1 teaspoon dried, crumbled)
2	sun-dried tomatoes, cut into small pieces
	Salt and freshly ground black pepper

Preheat oven to 475°F. Split the chicken down the back and flatten. Gently slip fingers under skin to partially separate it from the flesh. Do not remove skin; leave it attached to create pockets for flavorings. Sprinkle lemon with rosemary. Slip the lemon and tomato slices under the skin on the breast and thighs.

Brush the chicken with olive oil and season to taste. Place in baking dish that is only slightly larger than the chicken, breast side up. Roast for about 30 minutes or until done. Makes 4 servings.

Phyllo Chicken with Rice, Artichokes, and Cream Sauce

This recipe is a good one for a large group as it can be done completely ahead and then reheated before service. Add a mixed green salad and dessert for an easy-to-serve meal.

10	chicken breast halves, boneless and skinless	½	pound mushrooms, sliced
1	cup dry white wine or vermouth	¾	cup long-grain rice
1	teaspoon salt	¼	cup all-purpose flour
1½	teaspoons thyme	½	cup milk
½	teaspoon rosemary	1	package frozen artichoke hearts, thawed and drained, or one 14-ounce can artichoke hearts, well-drained
1	bay leaf		
9	tablespoons unsalted butter		
2	cloves garlic, minced	16	sheets phyllo dough
½	cup chopped onion		

Put chicken in a large pot and add wine, salt, thyme, rosemary, bay leaf and just enough water to cover chicken; bring to a boil. Reduce heat, cover, and simmer for 25 minutes or just until chicken is cooked. Remove chicken and cut into bite-size pieces. Set aside. Boil chicken broth, uncovered, until it is reduced to about 3½ cups. Set aside and prepare rice.

Melt 3 tablespoons butter in a small saucepan over medium heat and add garlic, onion, and mushrooms. Cook until tender. Stir in rice. Add 1½ cups of the reduced chicken broth. Simmer, covered, until liquid is absorbed, about 20 minutes.

Melt 3 tablespoons butter in a skillet over low heat. Stir in flour and cook until bubbly. Remove from heat and slowly stir in 2 cups of the broth. Gradually add milk. Return to low heat and stir until thick. Set aside.

When rice is cooked, stir in the artichoke hearts and 1 cup of the cream sauce. Set aside. Stir remaining cream sauce into chicken pieces. Set aside.

Preheat oven to 350°F. Grease a 9 x 13-inch pan with butter or cooking spray. Melt remaining 3 tablespoons of butter. Trim phyllo sheets to fit the pan. Brush 8 sheets with melted butter and place in buttered dish. Spread half of rice mixture over phyllo. Spread chicken mixture over rice mixture and spread remaining rice mixture over chicken. Butter remaining sheets of phyllo and place over top layer of rice mixture. Tuck in edges of last sheet and brush top with butter. Score lightly through top 3 or 4 layers of phyllo to indicate portions. Bake for 45 minutes or until golden brown and bubbly. Makes 12 servings.

Poulet Dijonnaise

Having a jar of Dijon mustard handy makes it easy to flavor many dishes. It's not related to the yellow ball park variety which would be a disaster in this dish.

4	large whole chicken breasts, skinless and boneless	4	to 5 tablespoons unsalted butter
	Salt and freshly ground black pepper to taste	½	cup imported Dijon mustard
		2	cups crème fraîche or heavy cream

Cut the chicken into 1-inch strips and sprinkle the strips with salt and pepper. Sauté chicken in butter over medium heat for about 4 minutes, until they are golden brown. Transfer the chicken to an oven-proof platter and keep warm. Stir the mustard into the remaining butter and juices in the pan, scraping up the bits. Beat in the cream with a whisk. Reduce the heat to low and cook the sauce until it has reduced by half. It should be thick and velvety. Adjust the seasonings and strain the sauce over the chicken pieces. Makes 6–8 servings.

Italian Chicken Breasts

If you have an oil mister, you can spray the breasts instead of using butter.
Be generous as the oil helps the breasts to brown evenly.

8	chicken breast halves, boneless and skinless	8	slices prosciutto
1	teaspoon salt	½	pound Provolone cheese, cut into 8 pieces
½	teaspoon freshly ground black pepper	2	eggs, beaten
½	cup Pesto Sauce (recipe follows)	1¼	cups toasted bread crumbs
		½	cup butter, melted

With a meat mallet, pound chicken breasts lightly to flatten to a uniform ¼-inch thickness. Season with salt and pepper.

Spread each breast with 1 tablespoon Pesto Sauce, and place a strip of prosciutto on top of the sauce. Place 1 piece of provolone cheese on narrow end of breast and roll up to form a cylinder, enclosing the cheese. Roll cylinder in beaten egg, then in the bread crumbs. Chill 30 to 60 minutes.

Preheat oven to 350°F. Place cold breasts on an ungreased baking pan. Pour melted butter over chicken and bake for 1 hour. Remove from baking pan and slice each roll diagonally into 3 pieces. Makes 8 servings.

Pesto Sauce

2	cups fresh basil leaves	½	teaspoon salt
4	cloves garlic	1	cup freshly grated Parmesan cheese
1¼	cups olive oil	¼	cup pine nuts or walnuts

Puree basil and garlic with olive oil in food processor. Blend in salt, cheese and nuts. Seal tightly with olive oil on top. Store in refrigerator up to three weeks or in freezer up to six months.

Provolone Chicken

This is an easy recipe that can be put together ahead and then popped into the oven just before serving. A little chopped flat leaf parsley on top would add some color to the dish.

5	whole chicken breasts, boneless and skinless
½	cup flour
3	eggs, beaten
	Seasoned soft bread crumbs
1	tablespoon each butter and vegetable oil
8	ounces fresh mushrooms, sliced
1	cup chicken stock
6	ounces white wine
8	ounces Provolone cheese, grated

Preheat oven to 350°F. Cut chicken breasts into scallops and flatten slightly with a meat mallet. Dust chicken pieces with flour, dip in beaten egg and roll in bread crumbs. Heat butter and oil in a skillet and sauté chicken pieces until lightly browned on both sides. Transfer to a buttered 9 x 13-inch pan, layering in rows, overlapping pieces.

Sauté mushrooms in pan drippings. Arrange over chicken. Add stock and wine. Cover with grated cheese and bake, covered for 30 minutes. Uncover and bake 15 minutes longer. Serve immediately. Makes 10 servings.

Breast of Chicken Marsala

A class demonstrating different recipes for cooking chicken breasts was one of our most popular classes ever. This recipe is delicious yet quick and easy.

8	chicken breasts halves, skinless and boneless
1	cup plus 2 tablespoons flour
2	eggs, lightly beaten
2	cups unseasoned bread crumbs
1	tablespoon butter
2	tablespoons vegetable oil
8	ounces fresh mushrooms, sliced
⅓	cup dry Marsala wine
1	clove garlic, minced
1	cup chicken broth
6	to 8 lemon slices
	Salt and freshly ground black pepper to taste

Dredge the chicken breasts in 1 cup of the flour and shake off the excess thoroughly. Dip breasts in the beaten egg and then in the bread crumbs. Melt the butter and oil in a large skillet; when it is hot and bubbly, add the chicken and sauté until golden brown on both sides. Remove the chicken from the pan and set aside.

Add the mushrooms to the pan and cook over medium heat for about 1 minute. Sprinkle the remaining 2 tablespoons of flour over the mushrooms and cook for an additional 30 seconds, making sure they do not burn. Add the marsala, garlic, chicken broth, and lemon slices. Stir the sauce until slightly thickened. Return the chicken to the sauce, season to taste, cover and cook over medium heat for 10–15 minutes. Makes 6–8 servings.

Chicken Piccata

Clarifying the butter keeps the milk solids from burning. This is done by melting butter and skimming off the milk solids.

8	chicken breasts halves, skinless and boneless
½	cup all-purpose flour
½	teaspoon salt
¼	teaspoon freshly ground black pepper
¼	cup clarified butter
1	tablespoon olive oil
¼	cup dry white wine
2	tablespoons lemon juice
1	teaspoon lemon zest, finely chopped
¼	cup drained capers
¼	cup fresh parsley, minced
6	to 8 thin lemon slices

Flatten chicken breasts to ¼-inch thickness. Combine flour, salt, and pepper in plastic bag. Add breasts and shake to lightly coat. Shake off excess flour. Heat butter and oil until bubbling and sauté chicken breasts, a few at a time, 2–3 minutes on each side. Drain on paper towels and cover to keep warm.

Pour off all but 2 tablespoons of the fat left in the skillet. Stir in wine, scraping the bottom to loosen browned bits. Add lemon juice and zest.

Return chicken to skillet and heat until sauce thickens. Spoon any sauce remaining in the skillet over the chicken. Sprinkle with capers and parsley. Garnish with lemon slices and serve. Makes 6–8 servings.

Stir-fry Chicken and Vegetables

Before Chinese food became so familiar, this was a favorite recipe of restaurant diners. Known as Moo Goo Gai Pan on most menus, you might recognize it. Instead of just stir-frying the chicken it is given an extra step called velveting, which enrobes the chicken with a light cornstarch coating, thus keeping it tender and juicy.

1	pound chicken breasts, boneless and skinless	¼	cup water chestnuts, sliced
½	teaspoon salt	½	cup fresh snow peas, strings and ends removed
1	tablespoon dry sherry		Salt to taste
1	egg white, lightly beaten	¼	cup chicken stock, water, or mushroom liquid
1	tablespoon cornstarch		
1	tablespoon vegetable oil	1	tablespoon soy sauce
1	tablespoon peanut or canola oil	1	tablespoon oyster sauce
1	clove garlic, minced	1	tablespoon dry sherry
2	teaspoons minced gingerroot	½	teaspoon sugar
2	cups bok choy, sliced (mostly white part)	2	teaspoons sesame oil
½	cup bamboo shoots, sliced	2	teaspoons cornstarch
1	(7-ounce) can button mushrooms, drained		

Cut chicken into 1-inch pieces and place in bowl. Add salt and dry sherry, and stir. Add egg white to chicken mixture and then sprinkle in the cornstarch, mixing well. Add the oil and stir until smooth. Let chicken marinate in refrigerator until coating adheres to the meat, about 30 minutes.

Bring 1 quart of water to boil, add 1 tablespoon vegetable oil and lower heat to simmer. Scatter in pieces of chicken, stirring to separate, and immediately remove from heat when coating turns white. Pour mixture into strainer to drain.

Heat wok or sauté pan over high heat; add oil and heat. Add garlic and gingerroot, stir-frying quickly so garlic doesn't burn. Scatter in bok choy and bamboo shoots and stir-fry about 30 seconds. Add rest of vegetables except snow peas and stir-fry quickly. Add salt and stock; even out vegetables and put chicken on top. Cover and steam-cook over high heat for about 45 seconds.

Add snow peas and stir-fry about 30 seconds. Mix cornstarch with 2 tablespoons cold water and add to pan with soy sauce, oyster sauce, dry sherry, sugar, and sesame oil. Stir-fry for about 30 seconds. Sample and adjust seasonings to taste. Serve immediately. Makes 2–3 main course servings.

Chicken Kuwayaki

This quick and easy dish is good served on a bed of rice. If you have leftover rice, you can add some vegetables for a quick fried rice.

½ cup flour
1   pound chicken breasts, boneless and skinless, cut into bite-size pieces
6   tablespoons salad oil
6   tablespoons water
9   tablespoons mirin or dry sherry
4½ tablespoons light soy sauce
4   teaspoons sugar
1   bunch scallions, trimmed and chopped

Sprinkle chicken generously with the flour. Add salad oil to a heated wok or skillet. Heat the oil and quickly brown the chicken. Mix the water, mirin, soy sauce, and sugar in a saucepan and simmer for 3 minutes. Pour this sauce into the wok, coating the chicken well. Cook over medium heat until the sauce thickens. Stir in the scallions and cook for 2 minutes. Serve with rice. Makes 3 servings.

Stuffed Chicken Breast in Sour Cream Pastry

This recipe came from a class I took at Johnson & Wales Culinary Institute.
It is fancy looking but quite manageable to do.

PASTRY:

1½ cups all-purpose flour

1 cup unsalted butter, cold and cut into small pieces

¼ cup sour cream

1 egg yolk

CHICKEN FILLING:

2 pounds chicken breast halves, skinless and boneless

1 pound spinach

8 ounces Italian sausage with fennel

1 cup finely chopped leeks

2 shallots, finely chopped

½ cup cooked ham, finely chopped

½ cup bread crumbs

¼ cup Parmesan cheese

¼ teaspoon dried tarragon

1 tablespoon parsley, chopped

1 egg, lightly beaten

Salt

Freshly ground black pepper to taste

Sauce Supreme (recipe follows)

1 egg, lightly beaten

Cut butter into flour with pastry blender until mixture is crumbly. Blend egg yolk and sour cream and combine with flour mixture, mixing just until mixture comes together. Wrap dough and refrigerate at least 1 hour before using.

Remove stems from spinach and discard. Blanch the spinach by dropping into boiling water; stir and remove spinach when just wilted. Drain and squeeze the spinach to remove as much liquid as possible. Chop spinach and set aside. Remove casing from sausage and fry until fat is released. Add leeks, shallots and ham. Cook over low heat until vegetables are limp and transparent. Transfer the mixture to a bowl and add the spinach, bread crumbs, Parmesan cheese, tarragon, parsley, and beaten egg. Stir well and season to taste. Refrigerate until cooled.

With a meat mallet, flatten chicken breast halves to about ¼-inch uniform thickness. On a large sheet of plastic wrap, place the breasts side-by-side, overlapping slightly. Place spinach stuffing on the chicken breasts and roll up.

Roll the dough out in a rectangle large enough to contain the stuffed chicken-breast roll. Wrap dough around chicken breast roll and tuck in the ends. Place seam side down on baking sheet. Refrigerate for 30 minutes before baking. Mix beaten egg with 1 tablespoon of water and brush over pastry. Bake in preheated oven at 375°F for 30 minutes. Serve with Sauce Supreme. Makes 8 servings.

Sauce Supreme

1½ cups chicken stock
½   cup dry white wine
¼   cup unsalted butter
¼   cup flour
1   egg yolk
½   cup heavy cream

Heat chicken stock and white wine until hot. Set aside. Melt butter in a saucepan. Add flour and whisk until mixed. Cook without browning, just until flour is bubbly. Add heated liquid and simmer for 10 minutes, whisking occasionally. Mix the egg yolk with the heavy cream to make a liaison. Add ½ cup of the hot mixture to the egg yolk and cream mixture to temper the egg. Pour back into the sauce and stir until well blended. Do not boil. Makes 2½ cups.

Lemon-Marinated Turkey with Golden Raisins, Capers, and Pine Nuts

Poaching a turkey breast is so much easier than roasting and the meat stays so moist. This recipe is great served at room temperature with the added bonus of its being low in fat.

½   Poached Turkey Breast (recipe follows)
3   tablespoons fresh lemon juice
1½ teaspoons balsamic vinegar
    Salt and freshly ground black pepper
½   cup olive oil
    Zest of 1 large lemon
⅓   cup golden raisins
2   tablespoons capers, drained
1   tablespoon finely chopped parsley
1   tablespoon finely shredded fresh mint leaves
3   tablespoons pine nuts, toasted and cooled

Soak raisins in boiling water for 5 minutes; drain well. Remove skin and bones from the poached turkey and discard. Place turkey in a shallow dish just large enough to hold it. In food processor bowl, pulse together the lemon juice, vinegar, salt, and pepper. With machine running, add the oil in a stream until the dressing is emulsified. Stir in raisins, zest, and capers. Pour the dressing over the turkey, cover, and refrigerate. Marinate, turning occasionally, for at least 4 hours or overnight.

Allow turkey to come to room temperature before serving. Slice turkey on the diagonal into ¼-inch slices. Arrange slices on a platter. Stir the parsley and the mint into the marinade and spoon over the turkey; sprinkle with pine nuts. Makes 4–6 servings.

Poached Turkey Breast

5½ to 6-pound turkey breast (with skin and bone)
1   large onion, cut into wedges
3   carrots, chopped
1   teaspoon whole black peppercorns
2   bay leaves
¼   cup plus 2 tablespoons white vinegar

In a deep pot combine the turkey breast with enough cold water to cover it by 1 inch and remove the turkey breast. To the pot add onion, carrots, bay leaves, peppercorns and vinegar. Bring to a boil and add salt to taste. Return turkey to pot and poach it, covered, at a bare simmer for about 1 hour and 15 minutes. Remove the pot from the heat, let the turkey cool in the liquid, uncovered, for 30 minutes. Remove turkey from liquid and drain well.

Steak with Green Peppercorns

Green peppercorns come in a small tin and are soft as compared to the dried ones we grind. A splatter screen confines the splattering on your stove as you sear the meat.

4   (6-ounce) boneless strip sirloin steaks, excess fat removed
     Salt
     Freshly ground black pepper
1   tablespoon vegetable oil
4   tablespoons shallots, finely chopped
½   cup dry red wine, such as Pinot Noir or Cabernet Sauvignon
¼   cup beef stock
1   teaspoon tomato paste
4   tablespoons green peppercorns
3   tablespoons unsalted butter
4   tablespoons parsley, chopped

Sprinkle the steaks with salt and pepper to taste. Heat the oil in a heavy skillet large enough to hold the steaks in one layer over high heat. Add the steaks and brown them on the first side for 3 minutes for medium rare. Turn and continue cooking until they are thoroughly browned, about 3 minutes. Remove to a plate and keep warm.

Pour off the fat and reduce the heat to medium high. Add the shallots and cook briefly until softened but not browned. Increase heat to high and add wine; cook until reduced to ¼ cup. Add the stock, stirring to scrape up and dissolve the brown particles that cling to the bottom of the skillet. Add the tomato paste, peppercorns and any juices that may have accumulated around the steaks. Continue cooking until the sauce is reduced by about half and stir in the butter. Adjust seasonings as desired. Spoon the sauce over the steaks and garnish with parsley. Makes 4 servings.

Grilled Beef Tenderloin with Balsamic Vinegar Marinade

This simple marinade uses balsamic vinegar both to tenderize and flavor while the olive oil serves to lubricate the beef. I like to serve Country Garlic Mashed Potatoes (page 162) and asparagus with this entrée.

1½ tablespoons balsamic vinegar
Salt and freshly ground black pepper to taste
½ cup olive oil
6 filet mignons, ¾-inch thick

In a small bowl whisk together vinegar, salt and pepper. Slowly whisk in oil until emulsified. In a shallow baking dish arrange beef in one layer and pour marinade over it, turning filets to coat well. Marinate beef, covered and refrigerated, at least 4 hours or up to 1 day.

Prepare grill. Pat beef dry, discarding marinade, and reseason with salt and pepper. Grill beef on oiled rack set 5–6 inches over glowing coals for about 3 minutes on each side for medium rare. Beef may be grilled in a hot well-seasoned ridged grill pan over medium-high heat. Makes 6 servings.

Filets of Beef Chasseur

This is another do-ahead company recipe that has seen a lot of service through the years. If you have two ovens, you could prepare this for thirty-two people. I like to serve orzo and fresh asparagus with this recipe.

8	filet mignons, 6–8-ounces each, 1-inch thick	2	teaspoons tomato paste
1	large clove garlic, minced	1	clove garlic, minced
1½	teaspoons salt	¾	cup dry red wine
¼	teaspoon freshly ground black pepper	1	cup chicken broth
		¾	cup beef broth
2	tablespoons olive oil	½	cup water
2	tablespoons brandy	¼	teaspoon Worcestershire sauce
2	tablespoons olive oil	2	tablespoons red currant jelly
3	tablespoons flour	½	pounds mushrooms, sliced

Preheat oven to 400°F. Make a paste of the garlic, salt and pepper. With hands, rub seasoning on both sides of the meat. Heat 1 tablespoon of the oil in a large, heavy skillet (not non-stick) until very hot. Add steaks, sear until brown on each side, but still raw in the center. Do not crowd pan. If oil begins to burn, decrease heat slightly. Repeat with any remaining steaks, adding oil as needed. Put steaks in a low-sided casserole, leaving at least 1 inch between each steak.

Add brandy to skillet. Cook over medium-low heat, stirring occasionally, scraping up all brown bits that stick to the bottom of the pan. Stir in oil and flour. Reduce heat to low and cook, stirring constantly, until mixture is golden. Stir in tomato paste and garlic; it will be thick and grainy. Remove pan from heat and whisk in wine, chicken broth, beef broth, water, Worcestershire sauce and jelly. Return to medium heat and bring to a boil, stirring occasionally, 10 minutes or until reduced by about ⅓ and thick enough to coat a spoon. Stir in mushrooms. Adjust seasonings. Cool completely.

Pour sauce over steaks in casserole. The sauce should come up no more than half way up the meat. Bake, uncovered, 15–20 minutes for medium-rare doneness, 20 to 25 minutes for medium to medium-well doneness. If baking two casseroles in the same oven, rotate them halfway through the baking time. Spoon some of the sauce over each filet when serving. Filets may be refrigerated, covered with foil, overnight. Bring to room temperature 1 hour before baking. Makes 8 servings.

Marinated Beef Tenderloin

This is the marinade I've used for beef tenderloin for years. I usually grill the beef, cool it to room temperature uncovered, slice it and serve it al fresco. I also omit the sugar when I want less sweet flavor. Cooling the meat, uncovered, before slicing ensures that the meat will stay rosy red. On the grill, sear and then cook over indirect heat with the lid down. We stop cooking at 145°F internal temperature, usually about 45 minutes after searing.

1	(5–6 pound) beef tenderloin
⅔	cup red wine vinegar
⅔	cup sugar
⅔	cup dark soy sauce
4	cloves garlic, minced

Mix ingredients and marinate meat for about 1½ hours. Remove meat from marinade and roast in preheated 375°F oven for 35–40 minutes, or on the grill as described above.

Stuffed Flank Steak

This is a great buffet dish with the colorful spiral of spinach rolled into the meat. Serving it at room temperture means you don't have to worry about keeping it warm for serving.

1	to 1½ pounds flank steak (not prescored, if possible)	½	cup Swiss or Gruyere cheese, grated
4	tablespoons unsalted butter	1	egg
3	shallots, chopped		Salt and freshly ground black pepper to taste
1	clove garlic, chopped		
4	ounces mushrooms, chopped	¼	cup fresh parsley, chopped
1	(10-ounce) package frozen chopped spinach, thawed	¼	cup fresh thyme, oregano or marjoram, chopped
1	tablespoon Dijon mustard	¼	pound pepperoni, cut into strips
½	cup bread crumbs	3	tablespoons oil
½	cup imported Parmesan cheese, grated	1¼	cups beef stock
		¼	cup vinegar

Preheat oven to 350°F. Butterfly the flank steak by slicing the meat vertically against the grain with a long, sharp knife. Heat the butter in a large frying pan. Add the shallots, garlic and mushrooms. Cook over low heat until soft. Squeeze the spinach until dry. Add to the shallot mixture, along with the Dijon mustard, the bread crumbs, the cheeses and egg. Season to taste, adding salt, pepper and herbs. Add more crumbs if necessary to hold together. Spread out the flank steak and fill with the mixture. Scatter strips of pepperoni on top of the filling. Roll up the steak like a jelly roll and tie at 2-inch intervals. Heat the oil in a large frying pan. Brown the meat well on all sides. Add the stock and vinegar. Cover with a lid and place in hot oven and cook for 1 hour.

Remove meat from pan, saving juices. Place a heavy pan or other weight on top of the roast to compress it so it will slice easier later. Refrigerate until very cold, about 8 hours. To serve, slice cold meat as thinly as possible across the grain. Serve hot or room temeprature. To reheat, place a little of the reserved juices in the bottom of a pan and add the meat. Cover and reheat ½ hour at 350°F. Serve with Mustard Sauce. Makes 6 servings.

Mustard Sauce

3 cups crème fraîche (recipe follows)
¼ cup Dijon mustard

Mix crème fraîche and mustard. Remix before serving if made ahead.

Crème Fraîche

2 cups sour cream
2 cups heavy cream

Whisk together sour cream and cream. Leave at room temperature overnight or until thick. Cover and refrigerate until needed.

Pot Roast with Herb Dumplings

The addition of winter root vegetables along with the dumplings gives this classic recipe a new look. The new generation of pressure cookers allows me to make this recipe in 30 minutes instead of the 2 hours in the oven.

2	pounds boneless chuck roast	3	carrots, peeled and cut into quarters
2	tablespoons flour		
	Salt and freshly ground black pepper	3	parsnips, peeled and cut into quarters
2	tablespoons vegetable oil	1	medium rutabaga or 2 medium turnips, peeled and cut into 1-inch wedges
1	medium carrot, diced		
1	medium onion, diced		
1	quart beef stock	16	boiling onions, peeled
1	cup red wine	4	medium red potatoes, skins on, cut into 1-inch cubes
4	sprigs fresh thyme or ¼ teaspoon dried		
		3	tablespoons olive oil
1	bay leaf		Herb Dumplings (recipe follows)

Preheat oven to 325°F. Trim excess fat from the chuck roast. Dredge the roast with flour and season with salt and pepper. Place a heavy-bottomed casserole on the stove over medium heat and add the oil. Brown the roast well on all sides. Remove the roast, add the diced carrot and onion, and brown. Return the meat to the pot, add the stock, red wine, thyme, and bay leaf. When the liquid comes to a simmer, cover the pot and place on the lower shelf of the preheated oven and cook for about 2 hours, or until tender, turning the meat once or twice during cooking.

Toss the remaining vegetables with the olive oil and season with salt and pepper. About 40 minutes before serving, place the vegetables in a roasting pan and roast in the oven until they are tender and lightly browned.

When the meat is done, remove the roast to a platter and keep warm. Strain the juices from the pot and skim off the fat. Return the juices to the pot and place on the stove over high heat until reduced by about half. Lower heat to a simmer and drop the Herb Dumpling dough by teaspoons into the pot. Cover and simmer for abut 10 minutes, or until a toothpick inserted into the dumplings comes out clean. Surround the roast with the vegetables and the dumplings. Pour the remaining juices from the pot into a sauce boat. Spoon a little over the meat before serving. Makes 4 servings.

Herb Dumplings

1   cup all-purpose flour
2   teaspoons baking powder
¼   teaspoon salt
2   tablespoons chilled unsalted butter or shortening, cut into small pieces
2   tablespoons chopped parsley
2   tablespoons minced chives
1   large egg
⅓   cup milk

Sift the flour, baking powder, and salt into a mixing bowl. Cut in the butter until the mixture resembles coarse meal. Stir in the chopped herbs. Beat the egg and the milk together in a small bowl. Add three-fourths of the egg mixture to the dry ingredients, mixing with a fork to make a stiff dough. Add the rest of the egg mixture if needed. Do not overmix or the dumplings will be tough. Cook the dumplings as above. Makes 15–18 small dumplings.

Roast Fillet of Beef
with Madeira Mushroom Sauce

The extra step of tying the meat helps it keep its shape while cooking. It also helps it cook more evenly.

1	center-cut fillet of beef, well trimmed and tied, about 1¾ pounds	2	tablespoons shallots, finely chopped
	Salt and freshly ground black pepper	½	cup Madeira wine
		½	cup beef stock
1	tablespoon olive oil	1	teaspoon tomato paste
1½	cups mushrooms, finely sliced	2	tablespoons butter
		1	tablespoon parsley, finely chopped

Preheat oven to 450°F. Sprinkle meat on all sides with salt and pepper to taste. Rub with olive oil. Place beef in a shallow roasting pan and put pan on bottom rack of the oven. Roast 25 minutes for rare (130°F), turning and basting once or twice as it roasts. Transfer meat to warm platter and cover loosely with foil to keep it warm.

Pour off fat from pan and place pan on stovetop, and add the mushrooms, salt and pepper. Cook, stirring, over medium heat until lightly browned. Add the shallots, cook briefly, stirring. Add the Madeira and cook, stirring to scrape up the browned particles in the bottom of the pan, until reduced by half. Add the stock, tomato paste and any juices that have accumulated around the fillet. Cook over high heat for about 5 minutes or until the sauce is reduced to ¾ cup. Swirl in the butter and add the parsley. Transfer the fillet to a cutting board and slice it on the diagonal. Serve meat on a warm platter with the sauce on the side. Makes 4–6 servings.

Stir-fry Beef with Asparagus

Stir-frying a small amount of meat with lots of vegetables is an effective way of reducing our meat consumption while enjoying its flavor.

1	pound flank steak, thinly sliced against the grain into 2-inch-long pieces
2	teaspoons cornstarch
1½	tablespoons dry sherry
2	tablespoons light soy sauce

3	tablespoons peanut or canola oil
½	pound fresh asparagus, washed and sliced diagonally
	Salt to taste
3	tablespoons chicken stock
2	tablespoons oyster sauce
1	teaspoon cornstarch dissolved in 1 tablespoon cold water

Combine cornstarch, dry sherry and soy sauce and mix well. Add meat and marinate for at least 30 minutes. Heat wok or stir-fry pan, add 1 tablespoon of oil and stir-fry asparagus until coated with oil. Remove asparagus from pan.

Reheat wok or stir-fry pan and add rest of oil. When hot, add meat and stir-fry until almost all of the pink is gone. Return asparagus to pan. Add chicken stock and oyster sauce and stir. Put on lid and let steam cook very briefly. Thicken with cornstarch mixture if desired. Makes 3–4 servings.

Sausage and Spinach Baguettes

This recipe can be made into baguettes, turnovers, or rounds. If the pastry softens too much, refrigerate for about 30 minutes before continuing.

2½	cups all-purpose flour	1	clove garlic, minced
1	cup unsalted butter, chilled and cut in small pieces	3	scallions, thinly sliced with some of the green tops included
1	cup small-curd cottage cheese	2	tablespoons parsley, chopped
1	pound Italian sausage, casings removed	1	egg
		2	egg yolks, lightly beaten
1	pound fresh spinach, blanched (or a 10-ounce package frozen chopped spinach, thawed)		

In a food processor or by hand, cut butter into flour until it resembles coarse meal. Add cottage cheese and mix until dough forms a ball. Knead dough lightly and divide into 2 balls. Roll out 1 ball into a 14 x 18-inch rectangle and about ⅛-inch thick. Cut rectangle in half lengthwise, then cut each half into thirds to make 6 rectangles. Repeat steps with second half of dough. Cover rectangles lightly and refrigerate while preparing filling.

Sauté meat until it is crumbly and no longer pink. Remove from heat and drain off fat. Squeeze spinach dry and place in bowl of a food processor; chop the spinach with the garlic, scallions and parsley, being careful to not overprocess. Add meat and 1 egg to spinach and process just until blended.

Preheat oven to 350°F. Grease two baking sheets. Divide filling into 12 equal parts. Spoon the filling along the long edge of each pastry rectangle. Gently roll up dough to form a baguette. Place baguettes, seam side down, on prepared sheets. Brush with beaten egg yolks and bake 20–25 minutes, or until lightly browned. Cool on racks. Serve warm or at room temperature. Makes 12 servings.

Grilled Pork Tenderloin
with Chipotle Marmalade Glaze

The sweet, hot and smoky taste of this glaze makes the pork tenderloin perfect for an entrée or sandwiches. Don't forget to watch them on the grill as the marmalade tends to burn.

1	cup orange marmalade
3	canned chipotles en adobo, with clinging sauce
2	tablespoons sesame oil
2	pork tenderloins (about 1 pound each)
2	tablespoons sesame seeds

Preheat oven to 350°F. Combine the marmalade, chipotles, and sesame oil in food processor and puree until smooth. Marinate trimmed tenderloins in mixture for 30 minutes. Toast sesame seeds in oven until golden. Heat grill and cook tenderloins until crisply glazed and cooked through but still slightly pink, about 15–20 minutes. Cut tenderloins across the grain at a slight angle into thin slices. Sprinkle with sesame seeds. Serve hot or at room temperature. Makes 4 servings.

Pesto Meatloaf

When I want this recipe, I usually don't have time to gather fresh basil and prepare it for pesto, so I always keep a jar of commercially made pesto handy in my refrigerator.

2	pounds lean ground pork Salt and freshly ground black pepper to taste	½	cup parsley, finely chopped and loosely packed
1	tablespoon olive oil	½	cup Parmesan cheese, freshly grated
2	tablespoons garlic, minced	1	egg, lightly beaten
1	cup fine, dry bread crumbs		Fresh Tomato Sauce (recipe
⅓	cup toasted pine nuts		follows)
1	cup fresh basil, finely chopped and loosely packed		

Preheat oven to 400°F. Mix the pork and salt and pepper in a mixing bowl. Heat the oil in a small skillet. Add the garlic and cook, stirring, until it softens. Add to the pork. Add the bread crumbs, pine nuts, basil, parsley, Parmesan cheese, and egg. Blend well.

Place mixture into a standard 6-cup loaf pan, pack it down and smooth the top. Bake about 60 minutes or until the internal temperature registers 165°F. Remove pan from the oven and let stand about 15 minutes before slicing. Serve with Fresh Tomato Sauce. Makes 6–8 servings.

Fresh Tomato Sauce

2   tablespoons olive oil
½   cup onion, finely chopped
1   teaspoon garlic, finely minced
2   cups fresh tomatoes, peeled and
    diced
1   bay leaf

½   teaspoon dried thyme
    Salt and freshly ground black
    pepper to taste
1   tablespoon butter
¼   cup fresh basil, chopped

Heat the oil in a saucepan and add the onions and garlic. Cook, stirring, until the onions are translucent. Add the tomatoes, bay leaf, thyme, salt, and pepper and bring to a boil. Reduce heat to low, cover and simmer about 10 minutes. Stir in the butter and basil. Makes about 1½ cups.

Chinese Barbecued Pork

Families in Chinatowns can purchase this already cooked. It is also used in egg rolls, for fried rice, and to garnish soups. Be sure to bring leftover marinade to a boil before using to accompany the meat.

2   pounds Boston butt pork roast
1½   teaspoons salt
1   tablespoon sugar
4   tablespoons soy sauce

2   cloves garlic, minced
2   tablespoons honey
2   tablespoons dry sherry
2   tablespoons Hoisin sauce

Mix all ingredients except the meat. Cut the pork into 1½-inch slices and place slices into a strong zip-lock bag and add the marinade. Marinate several hours or overnight, turning occasionally. Preheat oven to 400°F. Roast meat on a broiler rack over a pan with about 1 inch of water for about 10 minutes. Lower oven to 325°F and roast 30–40 minutes more, depending on thickness of the meat. Baste occasionally with marinade. Makes 4 servings.

Entrées

Honey-Gingered Pork Tenderloins

Pork tenderloins are great for two person families because they defrost and cook very quickly. One tenderloin usually serves two people. They are impossible to ruin unless you overcook them.

2	pork tenderloins, ¾ pounds each
¼	cup honey
¼	cup light soy sauce
¼	cup oyster sauce
2	tablespoons packed brown sugar
4	teaspoons minced peeled fresh gingerroot
1	tablespoon garlic, freshly grated
1	tablespoon ketchup
¼	teaspoon onion powder
¼	teaspoon cayenne
¼	teaspoon cinnamon

Pat pork dry and arrange in a shallow dish. Whisk together all remaining ingredients and pour marinade over pork. Turn pork to coat well. Chill pork, covered, turning once or twice, at least 8 hours and up to 1 day. Marinating in a zip-lock bag makes turning easy. Remove pork from marinade, reserving marinade, and arrange on a lightly oiled rack set 5–6 inches over glowing coals. Grill pork, basting with reserved marinade and turning every 3 minutes, 10 minutes total. Discard remaining marinade. Continue to cook pork, turning every 3 minutes, until 155°F, about 10 more minutes. Let pork stand 5 minutes before thinly slicing. Serves 4.

Farfalle in Salmon Sauce

This is not a recipe you can eat a lot of because it is so rich, but a small serving makes a good first course in a menu for entertaining.

8	tablespoons unsalted butter
5	ounces smoked salmon, finely chopped
1	small shallot, minced
1	tablespoon brandy
2	cups heavy cream
1	pound farfalle
4	egg yolks, beaten
1	tablespoon fresh chives, minced
	Salt and freshly ground white pepper to taste

Melt butter in a skillet over medium heat. Sauté salmon and shallots, about 2 minutes, until the shallots are soft. Add brandy and ignite (see note below). When the flame subsides, add cream. Cook over medium-high heat, stirring occasionally, until the liquid is reduced by half.

While the sauce is reducing, cook pasta in 6 quarts of boiling salted water until al dente, about 10 minutes. Drain in a colander.

Temper egg yolks by slowly adding ½ cup of hot cream sauce; blend well and return mixture to rest of cream sauce. Transfer pasta to a large bowl. Pour in the cream sauce and toss well. Sprinkle chives over top and season to taste. Makes 4 servings.

Note: In order to ignite, alcohol must be warm, so give the brandy a moment in the pan before lighting it. Using long fireplace matches to ignite the brandy will keep your fingers away from the flame.

Potato-crusted Salmon with Chive and Scallion Sauce

A good non-stick skillet is a must for this recipe. You have the entrée and starch all in one dish.

4	4-ounce salmon fillets, skin on	2	large potatoes, peeled and grated
	Salt and freshly ground white pepper to taste	1	tablespoon olive oil
4	teaspoons Dijon mustard		Chive and Scallion Sauce (recipe follows)

Preheat oven to 425°F. Pat the fish dry with paper towels. Season the fish lightly with salt and white pepper. Generously spread the flesh side, not the skin side, of each fillet with the mustard and with enough grated potatoes to coat entirely. Cover the fish with plastic wrap and press the grated potatoes down onto the fish very firmly and tightly. Remove the wrap and season the potatoes with salt and white pepper.

In an ovenproof, non-stick frying pan, heat the olive oil. When hot, place the fish very gently in the pan, with crust side down, using a large spatula to avoid breaking the crust. Sauté for 2–3 minutes until the potatoes are golden brown. Flip the fish carefully to the other side and finish cooking in the oven for about 5 minutes, or until the center of fillet is opaque in color. Place the salmon on serving plates and ladle some Chive and Scallion Sauce on the side. Makes 4 servings.

Chive and Scallion Sauce

1   tablespoon extra-virgin olive oil
5   scallions, thinly sliced, white part only
1   tablespoon chopped fresh garlic
¼   cup champagne vinegar
½   cup dry white wine
½   cup heavy cream
6   chives, snipped
     Salt and freshly ground white pepper to taste

Heat the olive oil and sauté the scallions for 2 minutes. Add garlic and when fragrant, add the vinegar. Let reduce until almost dry. Pour in the wine and let reduce until half remains. Add cream and reduce slightly. Remove from heat and add chives. Adjust the seasonings.

Cedar-planked Salmon with Maple Glaze

*Buy a piece of untreated cedar cut to fit your jelly roll pan, about
17 x 10 ½ inches. The plank can be rinsed, dried, and reused. Cedar
planks are quite commonly used in the Northwest region for cooking fish.*

1   cup pure maple syrup
2   tablespoons finely grated gingerroot
4   tablespoons fresh lemon juice
3   tablespoons light soy sauce
1½ teaspoons minced garlic
2½ pounds center-cut salmon fillet with skin on
    Salt and freshly ground black pepper to taste
1   bunch scallions, green part only

Preheat oven to 350°F. In a small, heavy saucepan simmer maple syrup,
gingerroot, 3 tablespoons lemon juice, soy sauce, garlic, salt and pepper to taste
until reduced to about 1 cup, about 30 minutes. Let cool.

Lightly oil cedar plank, place on baking sheet, and heat in middle of oven for 15
minutes. (Or lightly oil a shallow baking pan large enough to hold the salmon.)
Arrange scallion greens in one layer on plank or in baking pan to form a bed for
fish. In another small saucepan heat half of glaze over low heat until heated
through to use as a sauce. Stir in remaining tablespoon lemon juice. Remove pan
from heat and keep sauce warm, covered. Place salmon, skin-side down, on
scallion greens and brush with remaining glaze. Season salmon with salt and
pepper and roast in middle of oven until just cooked through, about 35 minutes
if using a plank or about 20 minutes if using a pan.

Cut the salmon crosswise into 6 pieces. On each plate arrange salmon and
scallion greens on a bed of Mustard Mashed Potatoes (page 154). Drizzle salmon
with warm sauce. Makes 6 servings.

Swordfish Skewers

This is a recipe I like to cook when I see a good selection of swordfish or tuna at the fish market.

1	pound swordfish, tuna, or salmon
1	medium red onion
12	wooden or metal skewers, 10 inches long
¼	cup olive oil
1	teaspoon ground ginger
1	teaspoon paprika
	Pinch of cayenne pepper
¼	cup chopped fresh mint
2	tablespoons lemon juice
	Salt and freshly ground black pepper to taste

Heat grill. If using wooden skewers, soak them in water for 30 minutes to prevent burning. Cut fish into ¾-inch cubes. Peel onion and cut into 1-inch pieces. Alternately arrange fish and onion on skewers. Brush with olive oil. Combine ginger, paprika and cayenne pepper. Sprinkle skewers with spice mixture. Grill over medium-hot coals 6–8 minutes, turning and brushing with more olive oil as necessary. Remove fish and onions from skewers. Sprinkle with mint and lemon juice. Season to taste. Makes 4 servings.

Mousseline of Scallops and Salmon

This is one of those recipes that would be impossible for the home cook to prepare without a food processor. Learning to effectively use this appliance makes many restaurant recipes manageable.

½	pound fresh salmon	2	tablespoons white wine vinegar
1	pound fresh scallops	½	cup Muscadet wine
3	eggs (1 of them separated)	¼	cup heavy cream
	Salt and freshly ground white pepper to taste	8	tablespoons unsalted butter
	Freshly ground nutmeg to taste	1	pound fresh spinach, shredded
2	cups heavy cream	1	(6-ounce) bunch fresh watercress, shredded
2	tablespoons unsalted butter, melted	1	teaspoon butter
1	teaspoon shallots, very finely chopped		

Preheat oven to 350°F. Butter 16 individual molds or small ramekins about 4 ounces in size. In food processor with metal blade, process scallops to make a paste; in a clean workbowl, process the salmon also to make a paste. Refrigerate scallops and salmon for 30 minutes.

Place scallop paste in food processor bowl with 1 egg, the egg white, salt, pepper and nutmeg. Process for 1 minute. Slowly add cream and process until blended, about 3 seconds. Transfer to another bowl. Place salmon paste in clean workbowl with the other egg, the egg yolk, salt, and pepper. Process one minute.

Spoon scallop mixture into buttered molds. Put salmon into piping bag with plain tip and pipe into center of mold. Place mold in shallow pan containing 1 inch of hot water; cover pan with aluminum foil pierced with small holes to allow the steam to escape. Bake for 30 minutes.

Put shallots, vinegar, and wine into saucepan and cook until reduced by half. Add

¼ cup cream and bring to boil. Whisk mixture over medium heat while adding butter in small pieces to create a butter sauce that coats a spoon. Remove from heat and adjust seasonings to taste.

Sauté spinach and watercress in butter for 1 minute. On warm serving plates, arrange some spinach and watercress in a small circle the same size as the molds. Unmold the mousse on the vegetables and top with some sauce. Makes 16 servings.

Shui Mai (pork & shrimp dumplings)

The addition of the chopped cabbage makes these bite-size dumplings moist and flavorful. My family can eat these by the dozen.

½	pound uncooked shrimp		Salt and freshly ground black pepper
4	water chestnuts		
2	stalks Chinese cabbage	1	tablespoon dry sherry
2	scallions	¼	teaspoon sesame oil
½	pound lean, ground pork	1	package of wonton skins, trimmed into rounds
2	tablespoons light soy sauce		

Clean and devein shrimp and chop with water chestnuts, cabbage, and scallions. Add pork and mix. Add soy sauce, salt and pepper, sherry, and sesame oil. Mix well.

Place a wonton round on the palm of your hand and cup it loosely. Place 1 tablespoon of filling on the wonton. With the other hand, gather the sides of the wrapper around the filling, letting the wrapper pleat naturally. Squeeze the middle gently to make sure the wrapper fits firmly against the filling. Tap the dumpling to flatten its bottom so it can stand upright. Repeat with remaining wontons. Place dumplings on a greased heatproof plate and steam over simmering water for 20 minutes.

Entrées

Scallop Timbales with Watercress Puree

The contrasts of colors and textures make this recipe an elegant first course.

1 pound scallops
1 cup heavy cream
2 egg whites
   Dash of Tabasco
   Salt and freshly ground white pepper to taste
   Watercress Puree (recipe follows)

Preheat oven to 350°F. Butter eight 4-ounce timbale molds. Place all ingredients into bowl of food processor with metal blade and process until the consistency of whipped cream. Fill molds with scallop mixture. Place in shallow pan with about 1 inch of hot water. Bake for about 20 minutes. Unmold on plate and surround with Watercress Puree.

Watercress Puree

1   bunch watercress, stalks removed
½   bunch scallions
½   cup chicken stock
½   cup heavy cream
½   tablespoon butter
     Salt and freshly ground white pepper
1½ teaspoons arrowroot

Place watercress, chicken stock and scallions in sauce pan and cook for about 10 minutes. Puree in food processor with metal blade. Add cream and butter. Season to taste and mix in arrowroot to thicken slightly.

Baked Shrimp Greek Style

By cleaning the shrimp yourself, you can avoid a water-logged product. Also, with the money you save you can be more generous with the servings!

2   pounds uncooked large shrimp, shells on
4   fresh plum tomatoes, about 12 ounces
6   tablespoons unsalted butter
3   large cloves garlic, minced
¾   teaspoon dried oregano
¼   teaspoon crushed red pepper flakes
    Salt to taste
¾   cup dry vermouth
3   ounces feta cheese
3   tablespoons fresh dill and/or parsley

Preheat oven to 350°F. Peel the shrimp, leaving the tail attached, and devein. Rinse under cold water and pat dry. Core the tomatoes, cut in half crosswise and squeeze gently to remove the seeds. Cut into ½-inch dice. Melt the butter in a large skillet over medium-high heat. Add garlic, shrimp, oregano, salt and pepper flakes. Cook, turning once, until shrimp are almost but not quite done, 3–4 minutes. Remove shrimp from skillet and transfer to a shallow casserole large enough to hold the shrimp in a single layer.

Add vermouth to skillet to deglaze the pan and cook until reduced by half, about 3 minutes. Add tomatoes and the cooking liquid to the casserole with the shrimp. Crumble the cheese over the top. (At this stage, the recipe can be prepared ahead, covered and refrigerated. Bring to room temperature before baking.) Bake shrimp until bubbly, about 15 minutes. Sprinkle with dill and parsley. Serve immediately. Makes 6 servings.

Strawberry Shrimp

The presentation of this dish can be beautiful with strawberries sliced to fan out around the shrimp. Be sure to use good-quality preserves so the color is bright red.

2½ cups flat beer
1   tablespoon salt
1½ tablespoons baking powder
1   tablespoon sugar
1¾ cups all-purpose flour
¼   teaspoon cayenne

1½ cups strawberry preserves
½   cup red wine vinegar
1½ teaspoons light soy sauce

¼   cup ketchup
1   clove garlic, minced
1½ teaspoons horseradish

2   pounds large shrimp, uncooked
¾   cup all-purpose flour
     Peanut oil
     Sliced strawberries
     Watercress

Combine first 6 ingredients, beating with a whisk until smooth. Cover tightly with plastic wrap and refrigerate overnight.

Combine next 6 ingredients in a pan and heat slowly until the mixture comes to a simmer. Remove from heat and let cool, or refrigerate.

Heat peanut oil in deep pan or deep fryer to 350°F. Peel the shrimp, leaving tails intact. Devein, split, and flatten. Lightly dredge shrimp in flour, then dip in batter and fry in hot oil until golden brown. Spoon ¼ cup of sauce on each plate and top with shrimp. Garnish with sliced strawberries and watercress. Makes 6–8 servings.

Cajun Shrimp

On menus in New Orleans they refer to this type of dish as barbecued. I never ordered it because barbecue in Texas is not like this. Don't miss out like I did for so many years.

8	ounces unsalted butter, melted
¼	cup Worcestershire sauce
2	tablespoons freshly ground black pepper
1	teaspoon Tabasco
1	teaspoon salt
½	teaspoon rosemary leaves
2	cloves garlic, minced
	Juice of 1 lemon
1	lemon, sliced
3	pounds raw shrimp in shells

Preheat oven to 400°F. Mix all ingredients except the lemon slices and the shrimp. Pour about ¼ cup to cover the bottom of a large baking dish. Arrange the layers of shrimp and lemon slices until 1 inch from the top of the dish. Pour the remaining sauce over the shrimp and lemon slices. Bake, uncovered, stirring once or twice until the shrimp is cooked through, about 15 minutes. Serve with French bread for dipping in the sauce. Makes 4 servings.

Spicy Fusilli with Grilled Shrimp

I like to serve pasta to large groups, but sometimes reheating the pasta at the last minute is not practical. This recipe is fine served at room temperature. In fact, like most pasta dishes they taste better if not refrigerated and reheated.

½   cup extra-virgin olive oil
½   teaspoon crushed red pepper flakes
1   tablespoon salt
8   ounces fusilli
1   tablespoon olive oil
16 medium shrimp, peeled and deveined
8   yellow tomatoes, peeled, seeded and chopped
1   cup chopped fresh parsley
3   tablespoons julienned fresh basil leaves
¼   cup toasted pine nuts
    Salt and freshly ground black pepper to taste

Heat ½ cup olive oil in a small saucepan; add red pepper. Set aside until cool. Strain oil to remove red pepper.

Bring a pot of water to boil and add 1 tablespoon salt. Cook pasta until al dente, drain and cool. Heat 1 tablespoon olive oil in a skillet. Add shrimp and sauté 3–4 minutes until cooked through, but still tender. (Shrimp may also be cooked on the grill.) In a large bowl, combine all ingredients and toss. Season to taste and serve. Makes 4–6 servings.

Artichoke Ricotta Pie

This recipe can be cut into smaller servings for an hors d'oeuvre or even rolled like a strudel.

¼   cup scallions, sliced
1   tablespoon olive oil
1   (14-ounce) can artichoke hearts, drained, squeezed, and cut up
½   cup sour cream
4   eggs, lightly beaten
1   pound ricotta
1   cup shredded Gruyere cheese
¾   cup freshly grated Parmesan cheese
½   teaspoon tarragon
     Salt and pepper to taste
     Olive oil or clarified butter
15   (8-inch-square) sheets phyllo dough (cut to fit pan)

Preheat oven to 400°F. Butter bottom and sides of an 8-inch square baking dish.

Sauté the scallions in 1 tablespoon olive oil. Add artichoke hearts, sour cream, eggs, all the cheeses, and tarragon. Season to taste with salt and pepper.

Brush each of 5 sheets of phyllo with light olive oil or clarified butter. Place sheets in baking dish and top with ½ of the cheese mixture. Brush 5 more sheets of phyllo with the butter or oil, place on top of cheese and top with remaining cheese mixture. Brush remaining 5 sheets of phyllo and place on top of cheese. Score lightly through the top layers the number of servings desired. Bake for 40 minutes.

Zucchini Moussaka

This Greek influenced dish is a refreshing change with its cinnamon and cream sauce.

1	pound ground beef		Vegetable oil
3	onions, chopped	1	cup grated white Cheddar cheese
8	tablespoons unsalted butter	6	tablespoons flour
4	tablespoons tomato paste	3	to 4 cups hot milk
	Salt and freshly ground black pepper		Salt and freshly ground black pepper
	Dash of cinnamon		Dash of nutmeg
12	to 16 medium-size zucchini	4	egg yolks

In a skillet, melt 2 tablespoons of butter over medium-high heat. Add meat and onions and cook until meat is no longer pink. Drain off excess fat. Add tomato paste, salt, pepper, and cinnamon to taste.

Cut zucchini lengthwise into strips. Heat vegetable oil in skillet and brown zucchini on both sides, working in batches. Layer zucchini in a greased 9 x 13-inch baking pan. Spread meat over zucchini and then sprinkle with half of the grated cheese. Repeat steps.

Make a white sauce by melting the remaining 6 tablespoons of butter over low heat. Add flour and cook, stirring constantly. Gradually stir in milk and cook until sauce is smooth and thick. Season with salt, pepper and nutmeg to taste. Temper egg yolks by adding a bit of the sauce mixture, then stir yolk mixture into rest of sauce. Cook for about 20 minutes. Pour sauce over moussaka, add rest of the grated cheese and bake in preheated oven at 375°F for 20 minutes. Makes 8 servings.

Gruyere and Onion Tart with Potato Crust

Whether you flip this tart out of the pan onto a platter or just cut wedges in the pan, it will get rave reviews at your next luncheon or brunch.

5	waxy or red potatoes (about 2½ pounds)		Freshly ground black pepper to taste
½	pound pancetta or slab bacon	2	tablespoons vegetable oil
2	medium onions, finely chopped Coarse salt and sugar to taste	3	cups grated Gruyere cheese (about ¾ pound)
3	cloves garlic, minced	5	eggs
1	tablespoon chopped fresh rosemary or 2 teaspoons crumbled dried	2	cups heavy cream or half and half Freshly grated nutmeg to taste

Boil the potatoes in water to cover for 5 minutes. Drain and cool for 10 minutes, then peel. Set aside to cool. Cut the bacon into ½-inch dice and slowly brown in a 10- or 12-inch oven proof, non-stick skillet until almost all the fat has been rendered. Transfer to paper towels to drain. In the remaining fat in the skillet cook the onions with a pinch of salt and sugar over medium heat until soft and lightly browned. Stir in the garlic and rosemary. Remove from the pan.

Preheat the oven to 350°F. Grate the potatoes with the shredding disk of a food processor. Season with salt and pepper to taste. Grease the skillet with the vegetable oil and press the potatoes against the bottom and sides of it. Place over high heat and cook just until the bottom of the potatoes begin to brown, about 5 minutes. Spread the onion mixture over the potatoes. Sprinkle with the bacon and Gruyere. In a bowl, beat the eggs with the cream until blended. Season with salt, pepper and nutmeg. Pour over the onions and bake for 30–35 minutes, or until puffed and browned. Allow to stand 10 minutes before unmolding or cutting into wedges. Makes 6–8 servings.

Penne with Summer Vegetables and Fontina Cheese

This colorful pasta dish is great summer eating. I use a pepper oil to sauté the peppers giving the dish an extra zing. Omit the pepper flakes if you do this.

1	tablespoon salt	2	cloves garlic, thinly sliced
1	pound dried penne pasta	3	large ripe tomatoes, peeled, seeded
1	tablespoon olive oil		and cut into ¾-inch dice
1	medium red onion, cut into slivers	3	tablespoons chopped fresh basil
1	medium red bell pepper, seeded		(or ½ teaspoon dried)
	and julienned	⅔	cup fontina cheese, cut into ¼-
1	small yellow bell pepper, seeded		inch dice
	and julienned		Freshly ground black pepper to
	Pinch of crushed red pepper flakes		taste
2	scallions, sliced	⅓	cup freshly grated Parmesan cheese

Bring a large pot of water to a boil and add salt and pasta. Cook until pasta is al dente.

Heat the oil in a large non-stick skillet over medium-high heat. Add the onion, red and yellow bell peppers, crushed red pepper flakes, and a sprinkling of salt. Cover and cook for 3 minutes. Uncover and cook, tossing with a wooden spoon, until the vegetables are crisp-tender, about 2 minutes longer. Add the scallions and garlic. Cook, stirring, until the scallions soften, 1–2 minutes longer. Transfer the vegetables to a plate.

Add the tomatoes and about half of the fresh basil or all of the dried to the skillet. Sprinkle with salt and cook, tossing until the tomatoes break down slightly and soften, usually 4 or 5 minutes. Before draining pasta, scoop out ½ cup of the pasta cooking liquid. Add drained pasta to the vegetables, tomatoes and enough of the reserved liquid to moisten the pasta and sauce lightly. Add the fontina and black pepper and toss just until the cheese begins to melt but is still in cubes. Serve immediately, sprinkled with the remaining fresh basil, Parmesan cheese, and freshly ground black pepper. Makes 4 servings.

Tomatoes Tonnato

This is summer eating at its best. When the tomatoes are in season and are ripe and juicy, serve this with a crusty bread for a light lunch or dinner.

4	ounces tuna, packed in water, drained and flaked	¼	cup olive oil
2	teaspoons capers, drained plus 1 tablespoon for garnish	1	cup mayonnaise
			Freshly ground black pepper to taste
3	flat anchovies, rinsed and patted dry	4	large, ripe tomatoes
¼	cup chicken stock	1	tablespoon grated lemon zest
2	tablespoons lemon juice	6	fresh basil leaves, julienned

Place tuna, 2 teaspoons capers, anchovies, stock and lemon juice in food processor bowl with metal blade. Process until smooth. With motor running, pour oil through feed tube. Remove mixture to another bowl and fold in mayonnaise. Season with pepper. Cover and chill until serving time. Cut tomatoes into ¼-inch thick slices. Arrange on serving platter, overlapping slightly. Spread the chilled tuna sauce over the tomatoes. Sprinkle with remaining capers, lemon zest and basil. Makes 4–6 servings.

Farfalle with Roasted Red Peppers and Fried Eggplant

The Italians choose pasta shapes to match the flavorings in the dish. The bulkiness of the vegetables in this dish would be too much for linguine or spaghetti.

4	Japanese eggplants, about 1¼ pounds
	Salt
1	red bell pepper, roasted, peeled and julienned
1½	cups olive oil for frying
¼	cup extra virgin olive oil
2	cloves garlic, minced
	Pinch crushed red pepper flakes
1	pound farfalle
¼	cup freshly grated Parmesan cheese
10	fresh basil leaves, chopped coarsely

Cut eggplants lengthwise into long, thin strips. Lay on paper towels and sprinkle with salt. Let sit for an hour or so while excess liquid drains. If using domestic eggplants, peel before salting. Heat 1½ cups olive oil in medium frying pan over high heat. Fry eggplant slices (do not crowd) until golden brown in color. Remove and drain on more paper towels. Cut into 1-inch pieces. Set aside.

Cook farfalle in boiling, salted water until al dente. Meanwhile, heat extra virgin olive oil in small sauté pan over medium heat. Add garlic and cook until lightly golden. Add red pepper flakes and turn off heat. Drain pasta and turn into bowl. Coat with garlic oil and toss in eggplant and red pepper pieces. Add Parmesan cheese and toss to coat. Sprinkle pasta with basil and serve. Makes 4–6 servings.

Sautéed Penne with Mushrooms

The method of sautéeing the pasta and adding the stock, risotto-style, makes this dish extremely rich tasting.

6   tablespoons olive oil
1   pound dried penne pasta
1   medium onion, peeled and diced
⅓   cup cognac
5   cups beef stock
3   ounces mushrooms, cleaned, trimmed and sliced
¾   cup heavy cream
½   cup parsley leaves, chopped
5   ounces Parmesan cheese, grated
    Salt and freshly ground black pepper to taste

In a heavy sauté pan heat 4 tablespoons of olive oil over moderate heat. Add the pasta and cook, stirring until it begins to brown, about 10 minutes. Remove to a bowl and set aside. Sauté the onion in the same skillet until soft but not brown, about 5 minutes.

Return the pasta to the skillet, stir in the cognac and cook until the liquid is evaporated. Add 2 cups of stock and cook, stirring until it is absorbed. Add 2 more cups of stock and, when it is absorbed, stir in the mushrooms. Add the remaining stock ½ cup at a time and cook, stirring, until it is absorbed each time and the pasta is al dente. Stir in the cream and salt and simmer until slightly thickened, about 1 minute. Remove from heat and stir in the Parmesan cheese. Sprinkle with parsley and freshly ground black pepper. Makes 8 servings.

Linguine with Tomatoes and Basil

This is a fun summer time recipe when Indiana tomatoes and fresh basil are abundant. I like to put the ingredients in a beautiful glass jar for the guest to admire before dinner.

4   ripe tomatoes, cut into ½-inch dice
1   pound Brie cheese, rind removed, torn into irregular pieces
1   cup fresh basil leaves, cleaned and julienned
3   cloves garlic, peeled and finely minced
1   cup plus 1 tablespoon extra-virgin olive oil
2½ teaspoons salt
½   teaspoon freshly ground black pepper
1½ pounds linguine
    Freshly grated Parmesan cheese

Combine tomatoes, Brie, basil, garlic, 1 cup olive oil, ½ teaspoon salt and the pepper in a large serving bowl. Prepare at least 2 hours before serving and set aside, covered, at room temperature. Bring 6 quarts of water to a boil in a large pot. Add 1 tablespoon of olive oil and remaining salt. Add the pasta and cook to al dente. Drain and immediately toss with the tomato sauce. Serve at once, passing the peppermill and grated cheese. Makes 4–6 servings.

Penne with Vodka and Spicy Tomato Cream Sauce

Authentic Italian plum tomatoes, especially those from the San Marzano area, seem to have more flavor than the American variety. They also seem to have less water so your sauce is thicker.

¼   cup extra-virgin olive oil
4   cloves garlic, minced
½   teaspoon crushed red pepper flakes or to taste
    Salt and freshly ground black pepper
1   (28-ounce) can peeled Italian plum tomatoes in juice
1   pound penne pasta
2   tablespoons vodka
1   cup heavy cream
¼   cup Italian parsley, chopped

In an unheated skillet large enough to hold the pasta later on, combine oil, garlic, crushed red pepper, and a pinch of salt, stirring to coat with oil. Cook over moderate heat just until garlic turns golden but not brown, 2–3 minutes. If tomatoes are not crushed, put into food processor bowl and pulse until roughly chopped. Add to pan, stir to blend, and simmer, uncovered, until sauce begins to thicken, about 15 minutes. Taste for seasoning.

In a large pot, bring 6 quarts of water to a rolling boil. Add 3 tablespoons salt and the penne, stirring to prevent sticking. Cook until tender but still firm to the bite. Drain thoroughly. Add the drained pasta to the skillet with the tomato sauce. Toss. Add the vodka, toss again and then add the cream and toss. Cover, reduce the heat to low for 1–2 minutes to allow the pasta to absorb the sauce. Add the parsley and toss again. Transfer to warmed shallow pasta bowls and serve immediately. Makes 6–8 servings.

Sides

Traditionally, most dinners are still composed of the classic meat, starch, and green vegetable combination. Some of the side dishes in this section will add a new look to your menus, especially at holiday times.

Zucchini al Forno

There's just enough breading on the zucchini to make me think it's fried. Baking means less oil and healthier eating.

2	tablespoons olive oil
2	pounds medium-size zucchini
2	large eggs
1½	cups fine dry bread crumbs
¼	cup Romano cheese, freshly grated
1	teaspoon minced garlic
2	teaspoons minced Italian parsley leaves
1	tablespoon minced fresh basil, or 1 teaspoon dried
½	teaspoon salt
½	teaspoon freshly ground black pepper
2	tablespoons olive oil

Adjust oven rack to upper portion of oven. Preheat oven to 375°F. Brush a large jelly roll pan with 2 tablespoons olive oil. Set aside. Scrub zucchini and blot dry. Trim ends. Cut lengthwise into ¼-inch slices, discarding first and last slices.

In a shallow bowl, beat eggs. In another bowl, combine all of the remaining ingredients except the olive oil. Dip zucchini slices in egg, then dredge both sides in bread crumb mixture. Arrange slices in a single layer in pan. Drizzle about ½ teaspoon of oil over each slice. Bake until slices are golden on top, about 5 minutes. Remove from oven and turn slices. Continue to bake until crusty and lightly golden, about 5–7 minutes. Using a spatula, transfer zucchini to a platter. Arrange in an overlapping pattern and serve immediately. Makes 6 servings.

Corn, Chile, and Cheese Timbales

The initial investment for specialty molds may seem like a lot, but if you have them you'll find uses for them. Individual molds make food appear more elegant.

1	(7-ounce) can whole-kernel corn with green and red peppers, drained
⅓	cup heavy cream
4	eggs
½	cup grated Monterey Jack cheese
3	tablespoons chopped green chiles
	Salt and freshly ground black pepper to taste
	Sour cream
	Chopped scallions
	Diced tomatoes

Preheat oven to 350°F. Generously butter six ½-cup molds. Coarsely puree corn and cream in food processor. Transfer mixture to a medium size bowl. Beat eggs, add cheese, chiles, salt and pepper. Mix well with corn mixture.

Divide mixture evenly among prepared molds. Cover each mold with a parchment paper round and place them in a pan with enough hot water to come halfway up the sides of the molds. Bake until set, about 25 minutes. Unmold timbales onto warm plates or serving platter by running the tip of a sharp, thin knife inside the edge of the molds. Garnish with a dollop of sour cream, green onions, and tomato. Makes 6 servings.

Chiles Con Queso
— Peppers with Cheese

This is a great side dish for a Tex-Mex buffet. The colorful melange of peppers brightens up a menu and the dish can be put together ahead and baked right before serving.

6	medium bell peppers (green, red, and yellow)	½	teaspoon dry mustard
2	tablespoons butter	¼	teaspoon freshly ground black pepper
2	tablespoons olive oil	¼	teaspoon cayenne pepper
1½	cups onions, thinly sliced	2	tablespoons flour
3	cloves garlic, minced	½	pound sharp cheddar, thinly sliced
1	teaspoon salt	4	large eggs
1	teaspoon cumin	1½	cups sour cream
2	tablespoons fresh cilantro, chopped		Paprika

Preheat oven to 375°F. Remove seeds from peppers and slice peppers in thin strips. Heat butter and oil in a heavy skillet over medium heat. Sauté onions and garlic with salt and spices. Add peppers and sauté over low heat for about 10 minutes. Sprinkle in the flour, mix well, and cook until all liquid is incorporated. Butter a deep casserole. Spread half the sautéed mixture in casserole. Top with half of the cheese. Repeat layers. Beat the eggs with the sour cream and pour over mixture. Sprinkle with paprika. Cover dish with foil and bake for 30 minutes. Uncover and bake for another 15 minutes. Makes 12 servings.

Brandied Sweet Potato Soufflé

This is a traditional Thanksgiving dish at my house. It is called a soufflé, but it is baked in a casserole for easy service.

3   pounds sweet potatoes
1   cup firmly packed brown sugar
8   tablespoons unsalted butter, at room temperature
8   ounces cream cheese, at room temperature
6   eggs, separated
¼   teaspoon freshly grated nutmeg
¼   teaspoon ground allspice
¼   teaspoon ground cinnamon
1   cup heavy cream
¼   cup brandy
    Salt to taste
    Confectioners' sugar

Preheat oven to 375°F. Scrub sweet potatoes and bake in the oven on a jelly roll pan until tender when pierced with a knife, about 1 hour. Cool, peel, and puree the potatoes. Transfer pureed potatoes to a mixing bowl, and add the brown sugar, butter, cream cheese, egg yolks, spices, cream, and brandy. Mix well. Add salt to taste. (This part can be made in advance, covered, and refrigerated. Bring to room temperature before proceeding.)

Beat egg whites until stiff and fold them into the sweet potato mixture. Pour the mixture into a buttered 9 x 13-inch baking dish or an oval gratin dish of similar size. Bake at 375°F until hot and slightly puffed, 35–40 minutes. Remove from oven and let cool 5 minutes. Sprinkle with confectioners' sugar. Makes 8–10 servings.

Basil and Pine Nut Bread Pudding

Tired of potatoes or pasta? This savory bread pudding makes a nice alternative to serve with grilled meats.

1	cup half-and-half
¾	cup heavy cream
4	eggs, beaten
	French bread, crust removed and torn into pieces to make 4 cups
	Salt and freshly ground black pepper to taste
1	small onion, finely diced
1	tablespoon chopped fresh basil
⅓	cup pine nuts
1	stalk of celery, finely diced

Preheat oven to 400°F. Combine all ingredients in a mixing bowl and blend well. The mixture should be very creamy. Add more half-and-half if needed. Pour mixture into a buttered 1-quart baking dish and let rest at room temperature at least 2 hours. Bake 45 minutes. Remove from the oven and cut into squares. Makes 6 servings.

Winter Squash with Roasted Walnut Butter

The combination of buttery walnuts with the squash is rich-tasting and colorful. The dish is just as good with all butternut squash.

1	cup walnut halves
½	pound unsalted butter, softened
	Salt and freshly ground black pepper
2	medium acorn squash
2	medium butternut squash
4	tablespoons unsalted butter

Preheat oven to 350°F. Toast walnut halves on a baking sheet for 15–20 minutes. Remove from oven and allow to cool before chopping finely. Combine chopped walnuts with the softened butter. Season to taste.

Peel squashes, remove seeds, and cut each squash into strips 2½ x ⅛ inches. Melt 2 tablespoons butter in each of two sauté pans over medium heat. Sauté squashes (the acorn in one pan and the butternut in the other) until crisp-tender, about 6–7 minutes. Combine squashes and toss with walnut butter mixture to taste. Makes 8 servings.

Stir-fry of Escarole with Pine Nuts and Garlic

Escarole is found with the lettuce at the grocery store. The Italians treat it more like a bitter green and sometimes add pasta to this dish.

5   tablespoons olive oil
2   tablespoons pine nuts
3   large cloves garlic, peeled and thinly sliced
1   large bunch escarole
    Salt and freshly ground black pepper to taste

Heat 1 tablespoon of oil in a small skillet over medium-low heat. Add the pine nuts and sauté, stirring constantly, until lightly browned. Reserve. In a large skillet, heat 2 tablespoons of the olive oil over medium heat. Add half of the garlic and half of the escarole and cook, tossing in the oil, until escarole is just wilted. Transfer to a side dish and season to taste. Add the remaining 2 tablespoons of oil to the skillet and cook remaining escarole with the remaining garlic in the same manner. Return the first batch of escarole to the skillet together with the pine nuts, adjust seasoning as desired, and just heat through. Serve hot. Makes 4 servings.

Corn Boats

After making corn boats for thirty-five people once, I decided that the boats weren't necessary to enjoy the superb corn flavor in this dish. By all means, wow your guests — but the boats don't hold enough filling because this recipe is just too good!

6	ears of corn, unhusked
5½	tablespoons unsalted butter
1	tablespoon chopped cilantro
⅛	teaspoon hot sauce
2	tablespoons mayonnaise
2	tablespoons fresh lime juice
2	cups grated sharp white Cheddar cheese
½	cup dry bread crumbs

Remove a lengthwise strip of corn husk, about 1–1½ inches wide, from each ear. Carefully peel back remaining husks, keeping them attached to stem ends and snap ear from stem end. Discard corn silks. Tear a thin strip from the tender inner piece of each husk and use to tie loose ends together, forming a boat. Cut corn kernels from ears and discard cobs.

Preheat oven to 375°F. In a large skillet, sauté corn in 4 tablespoons of butter over medium-high heat, just until tender, about 5 minutes. Stir in cilantro, hot sauce, mayonnaise, lime juice, and 1¾ cups of cheese, stirring until cheese is melted. Remove from heat and season with salt and pepper. In a small skillet, sauté bread crumbs in remaining 1½ tablespoons butter over medium-high heat, until golden brown, about 2 minutes.

Brush insides of husk boats lightly with oil. Divide corn mixture among the boats and top with bread crumbs and remaining cheese. Bake until tops are lightly brown. Makes 6 servings. (Note: Instead of corn husks, this can be baked in a dish: Put corn mixture in a buttered 6-cup casserole. Top with crumb topping and bake at 375°F until hot and topping is golden brown.)

Champagne Rice

This is a delicious side dish for grilled beef tenderloin with East-West flavors.

4	cloves garlic, minced	½	teaspoon Chinese chile paste
2	shallots, minced	½	teaspoon salt
3	tablespoons butter	¼	teaspoon ground cloves
1½	cups converted rice	1	cup dark raisins
1	cup chicken stock	½	cup scallions, minced
1½	cups champagne	⅓	cup fresh basil, chopped
2	tablespoons light soy sauce	1	red bell pepper, finely diced
1	teaspoon nutmeg	¼	cup sesame seeds, toasted

Melt butter in a pan over medium heat and sauté garlic and shallots until shallots are translucent. Add rice and sauté until coated with butter. Add chicken stock, champagne, raisins, light soy sauce, nutmeg, chile paste, salt, and cloves. Bring to a boil, cover, reduce heat to low and simmer for 25 minutes. Fold in scallions, red bell pepper, basil, and sesame seeds just before serving. Makes 6 servings.

Mustard Mashed Potatoes

*When I need mashed potatoes on a menu and I need to prepare them
ahead, I use Yukon Gold potatoes because they don't get as gluey when
reheated. If you want just plain mashed potatoes, just leave out the mustard.*

3	pounds Yukon Gold potatoes
1½	cups milk
6	tablespoons unsalted butter
3	tablespoons whole-grain or coarse-grain mustard
	Salt and freshly ground white pepper to taste

Put potatoes in a 5-quart pot and add enough cold salted water to cover the
potatoes by 2 inches. Bring to a boil, then simmer until tender, 35–45 minutes.
While potatoes are simmering, in a small saucepan heat milk with butter over
moderate heat until butter is melted. Remove pan from heat and keep milk
mixture warm, covered. Drain potatoes in a colander and cool just until they can
be handled. Peel potatoes and transfer to a large bowl. With a ricer or masher,
mash potatoes until smooth. Add mustard, salt, and pepper to taste, and stir in
milk mixture until desired consistency. (To make ahead, cool mashed potatoes
completely and place in a buttered ovenproof dish. Cover and refrigerate. Bring
potatoes to room temperature and bake, covered, in a 350° oven until heated
through.) Makes 6 servings.

Summer Squash Casserole

This is an ideal recipe for gardeners who find themselves with an abundant crop of squash.

4½ tablespoons unsalted butter
1   small onion, finely chopped
1   pound summer squash, trimmed, sliced ⅛-inch thick
½   cup grated Monterey Jack cheese
1   egg, lightly beaten
½   cup sour cream
2   tablespoons dry white wine or vermouth
½   teaspoon salt
½   teaspoon sugar
     Dash of Tabasco
½   cup fresh bread crumbs
1   tablespoon chopped fresh parsley

Preheat oven to 350°F. Melt 1 tablespoon of the butter in a large skillet over medium-low heat. Add the onion; cook until tender, about 5 minutes. Transfer to a bowl. Add 2 tablespoons of the butter to the pan over medium heat. Stir in the squash. Cook, tossing frequently, until all the moisture has evaporated and the squash is tender, about 10 minutes. Transfer to the bowl of a food processor and pulse until fairly smooth.

Transfer the pureed squash to a large mixing bowl. Add the cheese, egg, sour cream, wine, seasonings, and sautéed onions. Mix well. Pour into buttered 2-quart casserole. Melt the remaining 1½ tablespoons butter in a small skillet over medium-high heat. Stir in the bread crumbs; sauté until golden, about 2 minutes. Sprinkle the crumbs over the squash mixture. Bake until lightly golden, about 30 minutes. Sprinkle with the parsley before serving. Makes 4 servings.

Sautéed Cucumbers

Cucumbers are usually served raw, so it is hard to remember that they make a good side dish when they are cooked. I like them served with salmon or veal scallops.

2   large English cucumbers
2   tablespoons white wine vinegar
1   tablespoon unsalted butter
½   teaspoon dill
     Salt and freshly ground black pepper

Peel and seed cucumbers. Season with salt and sprinkle with vinegar. Place over colander to drain. Heat butter in sauté pan over medium heat and sauté the cucumbers for 2 minutes. Add dill and season to taste. Makes 4 servings.

Orange Marmalade Grapefruit

Being a Texan, I am a great fan of Rio Grande Valley grapefruits, but Florida grapefruits also work well in this recipe.

4   grapefruits, cut in half, at room temperature
½   cup good-quality orange marmalade
1   tablespoon Grand Marnier

Slice a bit off the bottom of each grapefruit half to prevent rolling. Place on a rimmed baking sheet. Mix marmalade with liqueur and spread on grapefruit halves. Broil until bubbly and browned.

Do-Ahead Mushroom Casserole

This recipe was developed to take advantage of the time-saving food processor when it first came out. I have to agree that slicing large quantities of mushrooms and onions is quick and easy with this machine.

¾ cup unsalted butter
French bread, crust removed
1½ pounds mushrooms
½ cup dry white wine
Salt and freshly ground black pepper to taste

Preheat oven to 325°F. Melt butter and reserve. Cube bread and process in food processor with the metal blade to make about 3 cups of soft bread crumbs.

Fit food processor with the medium slicing disc and process mushrooms, wedging them on their sides in feed tube so they will look like "chef's hats" after slicing. Place ⅓ of the mushrooms in a buttered 2-quart baking dish. Cover with 1 cup of soft bread crumbs. Drizzle with ¼ cup of melted butter and sprinkle with salt and pepper. Repeat the layers. Arrange the remaining mushrooms on top and season with salt and pepper. Pour the wine over all of this. (At this stage, the casserole may be prepared up to two days in advance; cover and refrigerate. Bring to room temperature before baking.)

Cover dish with foil and bake for 30 minutes. Remove from oven and top with the remaining bread crumbs and melted butter. Bake, uncovered, for about 10 minutes more or until top is golden brown. If not brown enough, place under hot broiler briefly.

Oven-Roasted Asparagus

This is easier than roasting asparagus on the grill if you are making a large quantity.

1   pound asparagus
1   to 2 tablespoons olive oil
    Salt and freshly ground black pepper to taste
    Freshly grated Parmesan cheese

Preheat oven to 500°F. Align the tips of the asparagus on a cutting board and cut off the thick, tough ends. Place the asparagus in a roasting pan in a single layer and brush with olive oil. Sprinkle with salt and pepper. Roast in upper third of oven for about 12 minutes or until tender, depending upon the thickness of the stalks. Season with extra salt and pepper as desired. Sprinkle with freshly grated Parmesan cheese and serve immediately. Makes 4 servings.

Broccoli in Hot Chile Oil

Commercial hot chile oil is readily available if you don't want to make your own. In fact, you might welcome another use for it if it is already in your pantry. This zippy combination adds a new dimension to broccoli.

2	pounds broccoli
⅓	cup olive oil
⅓	cup chicken broth
2	cloves garlic, minced
¼	teaspoon salt
¼	teaspoon crushed red pepper
	Juice of ½ lemon

Cut broccoli into 2-inch long florets. Peel the outer layer from the broccoli stalks and cut into julienne strips about 2 inches long. In a large sauté pan heat 1 tablespoon of the olive oil until hot. Sauté broccoli for 30 seconds. Pour in the broth, garlic and salt, and immediately cover the pan. Cook until just tender. Meanwhile, in a small saucepan heat the remaining olive oil with the red pepper. Pour over broccoli, tossing to coat well. Squeeze fresh lemon juice over all and serve. Makes 6 servings.

Baked Green Rice

Baking this rice in a loaf pan gives it an interesting presentation for a buffet table.

2   cups cooked rice
1   (4-ounce) can chopped green chiles
1   small onion, chopped fine
2   cups grated cheddar cheese
1   cup finely chopped fresh Italian flat-leaf parsley
8   tablespoons unsalted butter, melted
2   large eggs
1   cup milk

Preheat oven to 350°F. Lightly grease a 5 x 4-inch ceramic pâte or loaf pan and line the bottom with parchment paper. Combine the rice, chiles, onion, cheese, and parsley. Mix well. Add melted butter and mix. Beat eggs lightly, add milk and mix. Add egg and milk mixture to the other ingredients and mix thoroughly. Pour into the pan and bake for 40–45 minutes. Allow to cool completely, loosen sides and turn out onto a serving platter. Remove parchment paper. With a sharp knife, cut into slices. Makes 6 servings.

Glazed Shallots

Around holiday time, I like to double or triple this recipe so I'll have extras to use around the turkey or roasts. The shallots are also good sliced and added to meat sandwiches or added to peas or green beans.

2	tablespoons olive oil
12	medium shallots (about 1 pound)
	Salt
1	bay leaf
¼	teaspoon dried savory
2	sprigs fresh thyme (or ¼ teaspoon dried)
¾	cup dry white wine
¼	cup chicken broth
¼	teaspoon freshly ground black pepper
¼	cup chopped fresh flat-leaf parsley

Peel the shallots. Heat the olive oil in a medium saucepan and add the shallots. Spread out in a single layer. Cook over high heat, turning to brown on all sides, about 5 minutes. Add a pinch of salt, the bay leaf, savory, thyme, wine, and chicken broth and reduce the heat to low. Cover and cook until the shallots are tender, 20–30 minutes, depending on size. Remove shallots with a slotted spoon and set aside. Remove the bay leaf and thyme sprigs and discard. Bring the liquid left in the saucepan to a boil and reduce by half. Return the shallots to the pan and toss to glaze on all sides. Sprinkle with pepper and parsley. Makes 4–6 servings.

Country Garlic Mashed Potatoes

New potatoes are wonderful with just butter and freshly ground pepper, but occasionally this rich version is a treat.

2	pounds new potatoes, unpeeled, cut into large dice
1	tablespoon unsalted butter
4	or 5 cloves garlic, crushed
2	cups heavy cream
1	teaspoon kosher salt
½	teaspoon freshly ground black pepper

Place the potatoes in a large saucepan, cover with cold water, and bring to a boil over high heat. Reduce the heat to medium and cook until the potatoes are tender, about 15 minutes. Drain and return potatoes to the pot. Mash with a fork or potato masher.

While the potatoes are cooking, melt the butter in a small skillet over medium-high heat. Add the garlic and cook until garlic is just golden, 2–3 minutes. Add the cream and cook until it has reduced by half, about 7 minutes. (Watch carefully, as cream tends to boil over.)

Add the garlic cream, salt, and pepper to the potatoes and mix well. If necessary, reheat over low heat. Serve immediately. Makes 4–6 servings.

Spicy Cilantro Butter

This butter can be frozen if well wrapped. It comes in handy for a quick sauté or to top grilled foods.

1   or 2 jalapeno chiles, seeded, ribs removed, and finely chopped
3   cloves garlic, minced
1   teaspoon lime zest
1   tablespoon fresh lime juice
4   tablespoons chopped fresh cilantro
¼   pound unsalted butter, softened

Combine all ingredients. Lay a piece of plastic wrap on the counter. Put butter on top and wrap to form a cylinder. Refrigerate until you can slice the log. This butter is good on broiled fish, shrimp, squash, corn, or eggplant. It is especially good on corn on the cob with additional lime juice and freshly grated Parmesan cheese.

Desserts

There are almost as many recipes for desserts in this book as there are for entrées. What does that say about what most people like?

Whether you prefer chocolate or lemon, pie or cake, cookies or cheesecake, I believe you will find in this section a dessert recipe for every occasion.

Almond Madeleines

Madeleines are beautiful little tea cakes that make a cup of tea or coffee special. I like to serve these at the end of a Chinese meal when a little something is needed but not a rich dessert.

2	eggs, at room temperature
½	cup sugar
½	cup unsalted butter, melted
¼	cup toasted almonds, finely ground
1	cup all-purpose flour, sifted

Preheat oven to 375°F and butter two non-stick, 12-section madeleine molds. In a mixing bowl, combine the eggs and sugar. Beat with a whisk until thick, fluffy, and lemon-colored. Mix in the butter and the almonds. Gently fold in the flour. Fill molds two-thirds full with the batter. Bake for 20 minutes or until slightly brown. Remove from oven and lightly tap the pans on the counter; invert and unmold. Cool madeleines on racks. Makes about 24.

Amaretto Brownies

A quick toasting of the nuts really freshens and intensifies the flavors, especially if they have been stored in the refrigerator or freezer. These brownies freeze well.

½	cup sliced or slivered almonds, toasted	½	cup all-purpose flour
8	tablespoons unsalted butter at room temperature	¼	cup Amaretto liqueur
2	ounces unsweetened chocolate	4	ounces semi-sweet chocolate, broken in small chunks
¾	cup sugar	4	tablespoons heavy cream
2	large eggs	⅓	cup sliced almonds, toasted

Preheat oven to 350°F. Butter two 12-cup miniature muffin tins. Process almonds in food processor until finely ground. Set aside. Melt 4 tablespoons of the butter and the unsweetened chocolate in the top of a double boiler placed over simmering water. Stir until the mixture is smooth and shiny, 3–4 minutes. Set aside. Place remaining butter and the sugar in the bowl of an electric mixer and beat on medium speed until mixture is light and fluffy, about 3 minutes. Add the eggs, and continue to beat 2–3 minutes. Reduce the speed and add the melted chocolate mixture, flour, Amaretto, and ground almonds. Mix only until all ingredients are well incorporated. Fill each muffin tin almost to the edge with batter. Bake until brownies spring back when touched, about 15 minutes. Remove them from the heat and let cool for 5 minutes before removing them from the pans to cool to room temperature.

Combine semi-sweet chocolate and cream in a heavy, 10-inch skillet over low heat, and stir until mixture is smooth and shiny, about 3–4 minutes. Remove pan from the heat. Dip the top of each brownie into the chocolate mixture to coat lightly. Lift the brownie over the skillet and swirl it to let the excess chocolate drip back into the skillet. Garnish the top of each brownie with two toasted almond slices. Continue until all are decorated. Reheat chocolate over low heat if it gets too thick. Let brownies rest at room temperature until the glaze is set, 30–40 minutes. Makes 24 brownies.

Moravian Christmas Cookies

Make this dough several days ahead and refrigerate it so the spices can mellow. The paper thinness of this cookie is what makes it so unique and delicious.

4 cups sifted all-purpose flour (measure after sifting)
½ teaspoon salt
1½ teaspoons cinnamon
½ teaspoon ginger
1½ teaspoons cloves
1 cup plus 2 tablespoons packed brown sugar
1 cup shortening (can use butter and shortening combined)
1 cup light molasses
¼ teaspoon baking soda dissolved in ½ teaspoon vinegar

Sift first 5 ingredients together. Add sugar and mix well. Work in shortening with a pastry blender until mixture resembles coarse meal. Add molasses and dissolved baking soda. Mix thoroughly. Chill overnight. Divide dough into four portions. Work with one portion at a time, keeping the remainder refrigerated. Roll out as thin as possible on a lightly floured board. Cut into fancy shapes. Bake on parchment lined pans in preheated 350°F oven for 10 minutes or until lightly browned. Edges should not be overly brown. Immediately slide onto racks to cool. Makes about 100 cookies, about 3 inches in size.

Double-Chocolate Brownies

These brownies remind me of the truffles that we sell. They're more like candy than brownies if they're really cold. Whichever way you choose, they are intensely chocolate.

1	tablespoon butter, melted	½	teaspoon vanilla extract
2	ounces unsweetened chocolate	1	cup sugar
4	ounces semi-sweet chocolate	2	large eggs
8	tablespoons unsalted butter	¼	cup sifted all-purpose flour
¼	teaspoon salt	4	ounces pecan halves or large pieces

Adjust oven rack ⅓ up from the bottom of the oven and preheat oven to 325°F. Line an 8-inch square cake pan with foil. (To do this easily, turn the pan upside-down and place a 12-inch square of foil, shiny-side down, over the pan. Fold down the sides and corners to shape smoothly. Remove the foil and turn the pan right-side up again. Place the foil in the pan and press it gently into place.) Brush foil with the 1 tablespoon melted butter.

Place both chocolates and the 8 tablespoons butter in a heavy saucepan over moderately low heat. Stir occasionally until melted, whisk if necessary until smooth. Remove from heat, stir in the salt, vanilla, sugar and then the eggs one at a time, stirring after each addition until incorporated. Add the flour and stir briskly for about a minute until the mixture is smooth and shiny and comes away from the sides of the pan. Stir in the nuts.

Turn the mixture into the pan and smooth the top. Bake for 40 minutes or until a toothpick inserted gently into the middle comes out clean. Remove from oven and cool completely in the pan. Then place the pan in the freezer for about an hour until the cake is firm. Cover with a cookie sheet and turn the pan and sheet over. Remove the pan. Slowly and carefully peel off the foil.

Mark the brownies with a ruler. Use a long, thin, sharp knife to cut the cake into quarters and then each quarter into 4 brownies. Wrap individually for storage. Makes 16 brownies.

Walnut Spice Bars

This bar cookie is a nice addition to a holiday cookie tray because it offers a different shape and taste.

1	cup butter, softened	3	cups all-purpose flour
2	cups sugar	1	teaspoon cinnamon
3	eggs	1	teaspoon nutmeg
1	teaspoon baking soda	¼	teaspoon cloves
1	(10-ounce) package chopped and pitted dates	¼	teaspoon salt
		1	cup chopped walnuts

Preheat oven to 350°F. Cream butter and sugar. Add eggs, one at a time, beating well after each addition. Dissolve baking soda in 2 teaspoons of water and combine with creamed mixture. Add dates. Sift flour and spices together and beat into creamed mixture. Stir in chopped walnuts. Cover the dough with plastic wrap and chill several hours or overnight. Divide chilled dough into 6 equal portions for easier handling. On a lightly floured surface, work dough with palms into 10-inch ropes, about ¾-inch in diameter. Flatten the ropes with fingers to form a ½-inch-thick ribbon.

On an ungreased baking sheet, place 2 ribbons far apart (they will spread). Sprinkle tops with sugar. Bake on center rack of oven for 20–25 minutes or until light brown, dry on top, and barely moist on the inside. Cool about 2 minutes. While still hot, gently cut in half lengthwise, then slice crosswise diagonally into 1-inch bars. Remove bars to rack to cool. Cookies will harden as they cool. Repeat with remaining dough. Store in airtight containers. Makes about 12 dozen small bars.

Viennese Triangles

Our holiday cookie trays wouldn't be complete without this cookie. The shortbread crust, raspberry center, meringue and nut topping all contribute a layering of flavors. We cut the cookies into triangles and dip each side in chocolate — messy to do, but your guests will thank you!

CRUST:

2½ cups all-purpose flour

⅓ cup sugar

1 cup unsalted butter, cut into 16 pieces

1 teaspoon vanilla

1 egg

⅓ cup seedless raspberry preserves

FILLING:

5 egg whites

9 ounces sliced almonds

1½ cups sugar

3 tablespoons flour

1 tablespoon light corn syrup

1 teaspoon cinnamon

½ teaspoon almond extract

¼ teaspoon baking powder

CHOCOLATE DIP:

8 ounces semi-sweet chocolate

4 tablespoons solid vegetable shortening

Grease a 9 x 13-inch jelly roll pan. In workbowl of a food processor, combine sugar and flour and pulse to blend. Add butter and pulse until mixture is crumbly. In a mixing bowl, combine the egg and vanilla, and add mixture to flour and butter mixture. Pulse just until mixture is well blended. Pat mixture evenly into prepared pan and refrigerate for 1 hour. Spread preserves over entire pastry and set aside.

Position oven rack in lower third of oven and preheat to 350°F. Combine all filling ingredients, except almond extract and baking powder, in a heavy 2-quart pan. Place over low heat and cook, stirring constantly, until mixture reaches 200°F on a thermometer. Remove from heat and stir in extract and baking powder. Pour over pastry, spreading evenly. Bake until golden brown, about 30 minutes. Cool in pan on rack. When cool, cut into 1½-inch squares, then cut each square diagonally to make triangles. Melt chocolate and shortening in a double boiler and dip edges of each triangle. Set on rack to dry. Store in airtight container. Makes 5 dozen cookies.

Almond Ginger Cookies

When I was growing up, an almond cookie, especially one from Chinatown, was a special treat. This cookie is even better, and I can have one anytime!

2½	cups all-purpose flour	¼	cup honey
1	teaspoon baking powder	1	egg
3	teaspoons ground ginger	½	cup almond paste
½	teaspoon salt	48	whole almonds
¾	cup vegetable shortening		
1	cup light brown sugar, firmly packed		

Preheat oven to 350°F. Sift the flour, baking powder, ginger and salt together into a mixing bowl. Set aside. In a food processor workbowl with the metal blade, blend the shortening with the brown sugar, honey, and egg until smooth. Cut the almond paste into small pieces, add to the mixture, and process until it is smooth and the almond paste is incorporated. Add the flour mixture a third at a time, pulsing to mix, until a firm dough is formed.

Roll about 1 rounded tablespoon of dough between the palms of your hands into a ball. Place on an ungreased baking sheet and press an almond into the center. Repeat with remaining dough, placing cookies 2 inches apart on the baking sheet. Bake for 10–12 minutes or until the cookies are lightly browned. Cool for about 1 minute on the sheet, then transfer to a rack to cool thoroughly. Store in a tightly sealed container. Makes about 4 dozen 2½-inch cookies.

Lemon Bars

These are the best lemon bars we've found in years of trying different recipes.

1¾ cups all-purpose flour

⅔ cup confectioners' sugar

¼ cup cornstarch

¾ teaspoon salt

12 tablespoons unsalted butter, very cool and cut into 1-inch pieces

4 large eggs, beaten lightly

1⅓ cups sugar

3 tablespoons all-purpose flour

2 teaspoons finely grated lemon zest

⅔ cup lemon juice, strained

⅓ cup whole milk

⅛ teaspoon salt

Adjust oven rack to middle position and preheat oven to 350°F. Lightly butter a 9 x 13-inch pan and line with a sheet of parchment. Dot paper with some more butter, then lay a second sheet crosswise over it, allowing for overhang.

In the bowl of a food processor with metal blade, combine the flour, confectioners' sugar, cornstarch and salt and pulse to mix. Add butter and process to blend, about 8–10 seconds, then pulse until mixture is pale yellow and resembles coarse meal, about three 1-second bursts. Sprinkle mixture into lined pan and press firmly with fingers to cover entire pan bottom, about ¼-inch thick and about ½ inch up the sides. Refrigerate for 30 minutes, then bake until golden brown, about 20 minutes. Remove from oven and reduce heat to 325°F.

Whisk eggs, sugar, and flour in a medium bowl. Add lemon juice, lemon zest, milk, and salt and blend well. Pour into warm crust and bake until filling feels firm when touched lightly, about 20 minutes. Transfer pan to wire rack and let cool at least 30 minutes. Grasp the edges of the paper and lift the lemon bars onto a cutting board. Peel the paper down and off the edges, and use a sharp knife or pizza cutter to cut into 1½–2-inch sections, wiping knife or cutter clean between cuts. Dust bars with confectioners' sugar, if desired. Makes about 24 bars.

Lemon Macadamia Bars

George Geary, former pastry chef with Disneyland, has taught several popular dessert classes at our store. This one is my favorite from his lemon class.

2	cups all-purpose flour
¼	cup macadamia nuts, crushed
½	cup sugar
1	cup unsalted butter, softened
2	tablespoons lemon zest

4	large eggs, beaten
2	cups sugar
3	tablespoons all-purpose flour
½	teaspoon baking powder
¼	cup fresh lemon juice
¼	cup macadamia nuts, chopped and toasted

Preheat oven to 350°F. In a large mixing bowl, place the 2 cups flour, ¼ cup crushed macadamia nuts and ½ cup sugar. Mix to combine. Add the butter and 1 tablespoon lemon zest; mix together until well combined. Pat into the bottom of a greased 9 x 13-inch baking pan. Bake for 22 minutes, or until golden brown.

Meanwhile, in a mixing bowl, combine the eggs, 2 cups sugar, 3 tablespoons flour, baking powder, lemon juice, and remaining lemon zest. Mix until well combined. Pour on top of the baked and still hot crust.

Place pan back into the oven for 20 minutes. Dust with powdered sugar and the chopped nuts. Cut while warm. Cool and then serve. Makes 24 bars.

Baklava

Occasionally, only the sweetest, gooiest dessert will do, and Baklava certainly fills that bill for me. I usually flatten a muffin paper to hold each pastry piece before placing on the pastry tray.

1	pound walnuts, finely chopped
1	tablespoon plus 2 teaspoons cinnamon
1	pound phyllo dough
1	cup clarified butter
1	cup sugar
½	cup water
½	cup light corn syrup
1	cup honey

Preheat oven to 325°F. Use a jelly roll pan the size of the phyllo sheets, or cut the phyllo into a size that will lie flat into your pan. Brush pan with clarified butter. Bring to a boil the sugar, water, light corn syrup and honey. Remove from heat and let cool. Mix together the walnuts and cinnamon.

Brush butter over each of 8 sheets of phyllo, and layer them in bottom of pan. Sprinkle ⅓ of the nut mixture over it. Butter 2 more sheets of phyllo and place on top. Sprinkle with ½ of remaining nut mixture. Top with 2 more sheets of buttered phyllo. Sprinkle on the rest of the nuts. Butter and layer the remaining sheets of phyllo on top.

Lightly score the top layers of phyllo with a sharp knife cutting diagonally into 1½-inch diamonds. Bake 1 hour. Remove from oven and cool on rack for 5 minutes. Pour syrup over top. When cool, cut through bottom pastry to serve.

Biscotti

Along with the popularity of coffee drinks these cookies have become an American favorite. When we were traveling in France several years ago, we were told you could always tell the American tourists because they never dunked their biscotti in their coffee.

⅓   to ½ cup coarsely chopped toasted almonds
1¾ cups all-purpose flour
¾   teaspoon baking soda
¾   teaspoon baking powder
½   teaspoon salt
16 tablespoons unsalted butter, at room temperature
1   cup sugar
1½ large eggs
1   teaspoon lemon zest, grated
1   teaspoon orange zest, grated
1½ teaspoons vanilla extract

Preheat oven to 350°F. Lightly butter cookie sheet. Combine almonds, flour, baking soda, baking powder, and salt in medium-size bowl. In a large bowl, cream the butter and sugar. Add the eggs, beating well. Add lemon and orange zests and the vanilla. Add the almond mixture and mix well to combine. It will feel stickier and wetter than regular cookie dough. Form the dough into two 8-inch logs. Place on the cookie sheet, with at least 2 inches between them, and bake until the logs are just beginning to get golden, about 20–25 minutes. Remove from the oven and let cool slightly. Leave the oven on. When the logs are cool enough to handle, cut on the diagonal into ⅜-inch slices. Lay the biscotti on ungreased baking sheets, return them to the oven, and bake until crisp and golden brown, about 5 minutes on each side. Let cool on rack.

Lemon Bavarian Cream

A dessert buffet is a fun way to entertain. I always try to include a lemon dessert, a chocolate dessert and something with fruit in addition to others. This dessert looks lovely unmolded from a ring mold and the center filled with blueberries and mint.

2   envelopes unflavored gelatin
½   cup cold water
2   (8-ounce) packages cream cheese, softened
1   cup sugar
¾   cup fresh lemon juice
3   teaspoons finely grated lemon zest
1½ cups half-and-half
2   cups heavy cream, whipped
      Fresh mint
      Thin lemon slices

Soften gelatin in cold water. Stir the mixture over low heat until completely dissolved. Whip cream cheese until light and fluffy. Add the sugar, lemon juice, and zest. Beat until smooth. Stir in the half-and-half and the gelatin. Refrigerate until slightly thickened (about 30 minutes). Fold the whipped cream into the thickened gelatin mixture and pour it into a 2½-quart ring mold. Mixture can also be poured into wine glasses or individual serving dishes. Refrigerate until firm. Dip bottom of mold in warm water. Place a plate over top and invert. Garnish with lemon slices and mint. Makes 8–12 servings.

Coeur à la Crème

Individual coeur à la crème molds produce an authentic dessert with its heart shaped presentation. When we needed seventy-five molds, we cut PVC pipe into serving size, lined each with cheesecloth and drained them on screen wire.

1   (8-ounce) package cream cheese, softened
½   cup confectioners' sugar
2   cups heavy cream, lightly whipped
2   to 4 tablespoons Kirsch or Grand Marnier
2   (10-ounce) packages frozen raspberries in syrup
¾   cup red currant jelly
2   cups mixed berries
1   tablespoon fresh lemon juice
2   tablespoons Grand Marnier

Line 8 individual coeur à la crème molds with a double layer of cheesecloth, so that the cheesecloth extends 1 inch over each side. Set aside. In a mixing bowl combine the cream cheese with the sugar and whisk until smooth. Gently but thoroughly fold the whipped cream into the cream cheese mixture. Divide mixture evenly into each of the cheesecloth-lined molds. Place the molds on a jelly-roll pan and refrigerate overnight. Unmold the coeur à la crème onto a serving plate, peel off and discard the cheesecloth.

Thaw and drain the raspberries, reserving the syrup from 1 package. Place the raspberries in the workbowl of a food processor with the reserved raspberry syrup and red currant jelly. Process until smooth. Strain the puree through a fine sieve into a bowl and set aside.

Combine the mixed berries with lemon juice and Grand Marnier. Spoon berries and raspberry sauce around the base of each coeur à la crème. Makes 8 servings.

Basic Pie Pastry

Once you master pie dough in the food processor, you'll never buy premade products again. I make six crusts at a time and freeze them either rolled out or in discs. The recipe calls for butter, but you can use shortening or lard, as desired.

1⅓ cups all-purpose flour
½   teaspoon salt
8   tablespoons butter (or ½ cup other fat), frozen or very cold and cut into small pieces
¼   cup cold water

Place flour and salt in food processor bowl and pulse to mix. Add fat to bowl and pulse until mixture resembles coarse meal. Add only enough water to bowl to make mixture come together when pulsed. Do not overprocess. Put mixture into plastic bag and flatten. Put in refrigerator for 30 minutes before rolling out. Makes 1 generous 9-inch pie shell.

Peach Cream Pie

I make this pie only when Southern peaches are abundant. Because the filling is so creamy, the bottom crust doesn't stay crisp for long. I sometimes make a bottomless cobbler by weaving pastry strips across the top of the filling in a deep pie dish.

2   unbaked pie pastries for a 9-inch pie
1   cup sugar
5   tablespoons all-purpose flour
1   cup sour cream
3   cups sliced, peeled peaches
¼   teaspoon salt
2   tablespoons sugar
¼   teaspoon cinnamon

Preheat oven to 400°F. Add sugar and flour to sour cream and mix well. Mix in peaches and stir to blend. Place in unbaked prepared pie shell. Cut pastry into strips and cover peaches with strips placed in lattice-type fashion. Sprinkle top with a mixture of salt, sugar, and cinnamon and bake pie for 45 minutes. Putting the pie on a foiled lined bake sheet will make cleanup easier if pie bubbles over.

Macadamia Nut Tart

Unsalted macadamias are almost impossible to find locally, but that doesn't deter me from making this dessert. I just rub off excess salt with a tea towel.

½   cup sugar
1½ cups all-purpose flour
½   cup unsalted butter, very cold and cut into small pieces
2   egg yolks
1   teaspoon vanilla
1   cup packed brown sugar
⅓   cup unsalted butter
7   teaspoons each of pure maple syrup and light corn syrup
3   tablespoons heavy cream
8   ounces unsalted macadamia nut halves

In bowl of food processor, pulse flour and sugar to mix. Add ½ cup butter to the flour mixture. Pulse until crumbly. Beat eggs with vanilla and add to flour mixture. Process just until it comes together. Remove from bowl and shape into a disk. Wrap with plastic and refrigerate for an hour. Roll out and fit into tart pan with removable bottom. Refrigerate about 30 minutes, or until cold. Line bottom of pastry with foil and pie weights and bake in preheated oven at 350°F for 15 minutes, or until crust turns slightly golden. Remove foil and weights and bake 5–10 minutes more, until golden. Cool on a wire rack.

Combine brown sugar, ⅓ cup butter, maple syrup, corn syrup, and 3 tablespoons cream in a heavy-bottomed medium saucepan. Heat to boiling and cook for about 1 minute or until sugar is dissolved and mixture is caramel colored. Fill the cooled and baked crust with the nuts. Pour hot filling over nuts. Bake for 3–5 minutes, or until filling bubbles. Remove from oven and let cool on wire rack for about 2 hours. Remove sides of pan. Serve with a dollop of whipped cream, if desired.

Jack Daniels Chocolate Chip Pecan Pie

We're close to bourbon country, and this recipe shows that you can do more with whiskey than just drink it.

3   large eggs, lightly beaten
1   cup sugar
2   tablespoons unsalted butter, melted
1   cup dark corn syrup
1   teaspoon vanilla extract
¼   cup Jack Daniels whiskey
½   cup semi-sweet chocolate chips
1   cup whole pecans
1   10-inch pie shell, unbaked

Preheat oven to 375°F. Mix eggs, sugar, butter, syrup, vanilla and whiskey. Strain through a fine sieve.

Sprinkle chocolate chips over bottom of pie shell, cover with pecans and pour strained filling over all. Place in preheated oven and bake for 35–40 minutes or until knife inserted halfway between center and the edge comes out clean. Let stand 30 minutes before cutting.

Prize-Winning Apple Pie

This recipe was given to me by a California friend and credit must be given to her for its winning First Prize at the Apple Festival held at Donner Park in 1976. My favorite apples for this pie are Jonathan or Granny Smith.

1	9-inch unbaked pie crust
8	cups apples (peeled and thinly sliced)
¾	cup sugar
½	cup all-purpose flour
¼	teaspoon salt
1	teaspoon cinnamon
1	cup heavy cream
3	tablespoons unsalted butter
2	tablespoons light brown sugar

Preheat oven to 400°F. Line the pie crust with the apple slices, mounding in the center. Combine the sugar, ¼ cup flour, salt, and cinnamon. Whisk in the cream and pour the mixture over the apples.

Combine the remaining ¼ cup flour, butter, and brown sugar and sprinkle over the top of the pie. Bake for 1 hour.

French Apple Tart

This easy tart will look like it is right out of the food magazines. You don't have to tell how simple it is to make when your guests rave.

2¼ cups all-purpose flour

¾ cup sugar

1 cup unsalted butter, room temperature

2 tablespoons cider vinegar

2 tablespoons water

3 large Granny Smith apples, peeled and thinly sliced

1 tablespoon all-purpose flour

2 teaspoons cornstarch

¼ cup cold water

1 tablespoon lemon juice

½ teaspoon cinnamon

Combine the flour and ¼ cup sugar. Blend in butter with a fork or pastry blender, until mixture resembles coarse meal. Combine the vinegar and water and sprinkle over the butter and flour, stirring well until a soft dough is formed. Press into a 9-inch fluted tart pan. (It may also be rolled out with a rolling pin.)

Arrange apple slices over crust, slightly overlapping the slices as you work around the outside circle. Similarly, form an inner circle of overlapping slices. Repeat, forming two layers of thinly sliced apples in a circular pattern. Combine the 1 tablespoon flour and ¼ cup sugar, and sprinkle this over the top layer of apples. Bake in preheated oven at 350°F for about 25–30 minutes. Apples should be tender and slightly brown at the edges.

Mix cornstarch with cold water, then add remaining sugar, lemon juice, and cinnamon. Heat over medium heat, stirring constantly until thickened. Remove from heat. Brush warm glaze onto warm tart to give it an even, shiny brown topping. Let cool before serving.

Pumpkin Pecan Rum Pie

I know from experience not to venture too far from traditional holiday foods, but this variation just makes pumpkin pie tastier.

	Pastry for 9-inch pie crust	¼	teaspoon freshly grated nutmeg
1	cup coarsely chopped pecans	1	cup canned pumpkin
½	cup firmly packed light brown sugar	⅔	cup firmly packed light brown sugar
3	tablespoons unsalted butter, room temperature	2	eggs
		3	tablespoons dark rum
⅛	teaspoon salt		
		1	cup heavy cream
1	cup evaporated milk	2	tablespoons confectioners' sugar
1	teaspoon cinnamon	1	teaspoon dark rum
½	teaspoon salt	½	cup Honey-glazed Pecans (recipe
½	teaspoon ginger		follows)
¼	teaspoon cloves		

Preheat oven to 450°F. Roll out pastry and fit into 9-inch tart pan with removable bottom. Line pastry with parchment paper and pie weights and bake for 10 minutes. Remove weights and paper.

Mix the pecans, ½ cup brown sugar, butter, and ⅛ teaspoon salt. Spread mixture in bottom of crust. Blend milk, cinnamon, ½ teaspoon salt, ginger, cloves, and nutmeg in a large bowl. Add the pumpkin, ⅔ cup brown sugar, eggs, and 3 tablespoons rum and blend well. Carefully spoon pumpkin mixture into crust. Place on baking sheet. Bake 10 minutes. Reduce oven temperature to 350°F and continue baking until filling is set (about 35–45 minutes). Cool on baking sheet 15 minutes. Transfer pie to wire rack to cool completely.

Remove pan sides and place pie on serving dish. Whip cream, add confectioners' sugar and 1 teaspoon rum. Pipe decorative border around the edge and arrange Honey-glazed pecans on the cream border.

Honey-glazed Pecans

1   cup pecan halves
¾   cup water
¼   cup honey
3   tablespoons sugar
1   cup vegetable oil

Combine pecans, water and honey in a heavy 1 quart pan. Bring to boil over medium-high heat and boil 5 minutes. Quickly drain through sieve, discarding liquid. Return pecans to empty pan. Place over medium heat and sprinkle pecans with sugar. Immediately remove pan from heat and toss pecans to coat thoroughly with sugar. Arrange in single layer on waxed paper. Dry at least 15 minutes.

Heat oil in a deep pan over medium-high heat to 375°F. Deep fry pecans in the hot oil, stirring until just light brown and sugar begins to caramelize, about 2 minutes. Using slotted spoon, quickly transfer pecans to absorbent kitchen towel (do not use paper) and drain. Do not let pecans touch each other. Cool until crisp and dry. Pecans can be stored in an air-tight container for up to 1 week. Makes 1 cup.

Pumpkin Pie

This is the other traditional holiday pie at our house. It combines just the right amount of spice for our family. Although I just serve whipped cream with it, you might want to dress it up with the Pecan Ring (recipe following).

1	cup firmly packed brown sugar	¼	teaspoon ground cloves
1	tablespoon all-purpose flour	2	cups canned pumpkin
½	teaspoon salt	1⅔	cups evaporated milk
1¼	teaspoons cinnamon	1	egg, slightly beaten
½	teaspoon nutmeg	1	9-inch pie shell, unbaked
½	teaspoon ginger		

Preheat oven to 425°F. Combine first 7 ingredients. Mix pumpkin, milk, and egg. Add the dry ingredients and stir until smooth. Pour into pie shell and bake for 15 minutes. Reduce heat to 350°F and bake for 45 minutes more, or until done.

Pecan Ring

½ cup pecans, coarsely chopped
2 tablespoons brown sugar
1 tablespoon butter
1½ teaspoons grated orange zest

Combine all ingredients. Fifteen minutes before the pie is done, spoon mixture on the pie in a circle around the edge. Return pie to oven to finish baking as above.

Pecan Pie

Although this is a classic pecan pie, it is affectionally known as "Susie's pecan pie" in our family. She was the first to serve it to our family at Thanksgiving. We always have it at holiday time.

¼	cup butter
1	cup light brown sugar
1	cup white corn syrup
3	eggs
	Pinch of salt
1	teaspoon vanilla
1	cup pecans
1	9-inch pie shell, unbaked

Preheat oven to 350°F. Cream butter; add sugar and syrup and blend well. Beat eggs until light and fluffy. Add salt. Add eggs to butter and sugar mixture. Add vanilla, blend well, and stir in nuts. Pour mixture into pie shell and bake for 50 minutes or until done.

Cranberry Walnut Strudel

This is a great do-ahead holiday dessert that can be frozen in anticpation of holiday entertaining. It also makes a nice breakfast pastry.

1¼	cups plus 2 tablespoons sugar	6	sheets phyllo dough
½	cup plus 1½ tablespoons water	8	tablespoons unsalted butter, melted and clarified
4	cups cranberries, picked over and rinsed	¼	cup dry bread crumbs or cookie crumbs
½	cup raisins		
1	teaspoon finely chopped gingerroot	1½	cups heavy cream
		1½	teaspoons vanilla extract
1	tablespoon cornstarch	2	tablespoons confectioners' sugar
1	cup walnuts, coarsely chopped		

Combine 1 cup plus 2 tablespoons of the sugar with ½ cup water in a large, heavy saucepan. Place pan over medium heat and stir to dissolve the sugar. Add 2 cups of the cranberries, the raisins, and the gingerroot. Cook, stirring, until the berries pop, 5–6 minutes. Remove from heat. Combine cornstarch with remaining 1½ tablespoons water and stir mixture and remaining 2 cups of berries into the cooked berries. Return pan to heat and cook, stirring, until mixture has thickened, 2–3 minutes. Remove from heat and stir in the walnuts. Let cool.

Preheat oven to 375°F. Brush each of 3 phyllo sheets generously with clarified butter and sprinkle with 1 tablespoon each of bread or cookie crumbs and sugar. Place half the cooled cranberry mixture on the end of the phyllo sheet nearest you and spread the filling horizontally to form a 3-inch wide strip, going almost to the edges. Fold the two long sides of the dough over about 1½ inches to enclose some of the filling. Starting at the end with the filling, roll the dough into a log shape. Butter a jelly roll pan. Using two spatulas, transfer strudel to the pan. Brush the strudel with melted butter. Repeat for the second strudel. Bake 20 minutes or until strudel is golden. Allow to cool for 5 minutes before slicing.

Whip cream until soft mounds form. Add the vanilla and 2 tablespoons confectioners' sugar and whip until firm. Serve with warm or room temperature strudel slices. Makes 10–12 servings.

Puff Pastry with Preserves

This quick and easy dessert can be put together in no time if you keep the dough on hand in your freezer and have preserves in your pantry. It adds variety to a breakfast buffet without too much time and effort.

1   pound frozen puff pastry, thawed
½   cup strawberry or raspberry preserves
1   egg white

Roll out puff pastry dough on a floured surface to an 8 x 12-inch rectangle about ¼-inch thick. Trim the edges and cut the rectangle in half lengthwise to make two 4 x 12-inch strips. Lightly sprinkle a baking sheet with water and place one strip on it. Spoon the preserves down the center of the dough.

Fold the other strip in half lengthwise and cut across the fold with a sharp knife at ¼-inch intervals, taking care to stop within ½-inch of the edge. Brush the edges of the first strip of dough with cold water, and set the cut piece on top with the fold in the center. Unfold the dough and press the edges of the two strips together, enclosing the preserves. Chill for at least 15 minutes. (At this point, the pastry can be made up to a day ahead and refrigerated. It can also be frozen; defrost in refrigerator before baking.)

Bake the pastry in preheated oven at 425°F for 8 minutes. Lower heat to 375°F and continue baking until puffed and brown, 20–25 minutes. About 10 minutes before the end of the baking, beat the egg white until frothy, brush the top of the pastry with it, and sprinkle generously with sugar. Serve warm or at room temperature. Makes 4–6 servings.

Christmas Cheesecake

Don't skip this recipe just because it has candied fruit like a fruitcake. It is fun to serve at holiday time, and it looks lovely on a dessert table decorated in the spirit of the season. The cheesecake is best made one or two days ahead.

1	cup pecans, finely ground
1	cup graham cracker crumbs
1	cup confectioners' sugar
8	tablespoons unsalted butter, melted
½	cup mixed candied fruits, coarsely chopped
½	cup raisins
½	cup Kirsch
3	(8-ounce) packages cream cheese, at room temperature
1	cup sugar
4	large eggs
1	pint sour cream
½	cup sugar
	Pecan halves
	Candied cherries

Toss the pecans, graham cracker crumbs and confectioners' sugar in a medium-size bowl. Add melted butter and mix well with a fork. Firmly pack mixture evenly on the bottom of a 10-inch springform pan and set aside.

Place the candied fruits and raisins in a small bowl and cover with the Kirsch and marinate 1 hour or longer.

Place oven rack in the center of oven and preheat oven to 300°F. In the bowl of an electric mixer, beat the cream cheese and 1 cup of sugar together until the mixture is smooth. Add the eggs and mix just until eggs are incorporated. Drain the fruits and fold them into the cream cheese mixture. Pour the mixture over the graham cracker crumb crust. Place a rimmed baking sheet under the pan to catch any drips and bake cheesecake until firm, 50–55 minutes. Remove from oven.

Whisk the sour cream and remaining sugar together in a small bowl. Using an icing spatula, spread the topping over the warm cheesecake. Return the cheesecake to the oven and bake until the topping is set, about 10 minutes. Remove the cheesecake from the oven and let it cool to room temperature. Cover with plastic wrap and refrigerate overnight. Store covered and refrigerated. To serve, remove sides from springform pan and decorate the cheesecake with a border of pecan halves and candied cherries. Makes 12–14 servings.

Pagliacci's New York Cheesecake

*My favorite variation of this cheesecake is to omit the crust and bake in a
10 x 3-inch cake pan lined with a round of parchment. Put this pan into a
hot water bath and bake as directed. When cold, it can be unmolded and
frosted with White Chocolate Cream Cheese Buttercream. Setting the cold
cake pan on hot towels usually loosens the bottom enough for a clean
unmolding.*

1¼ cups finely ground graham cracker crumbs
¼   cup sugar
¼   cup unsalted butter, at room temperature
5   (8-ounce) packages cream cheese, at room temperature
2   tablespoons fresh lemon juice
2   teaspoons vanilla extract
1¾ cups sugar
3   tablespoons all-purpose flour
¼   teaspoon salt
5   eggs
2   egg yolks
¼   cup heavy cream
    White Chocolate Cream Cheese Buttercream (recipe follows)

Mix crumbs, ¼ cup sugar, and butter until mixture resembles coarse meal. Press
firmly into bottom and ½-inch up sides of 9-inch springform pan. Refrigerate
until ready to use.

Preheat oven to 500°F. Beat cream cheese in large bowl with electric mixer until
very smooth. Blend in lemon juice and vanilla extract. Sift together sugar, flour
and salt. Gradually beat into cream cheese, then continue beating until mixture is
creamy, smooth and light, about 5 minutes. Beat in eggs and yolks one at a time,
beating lightly after each addition. Beat in cream. Pour into crust. Bake 12

minutes. Reduce oven temperature to 300°F. Continue baking until tester, inserted in center of cake comes out clean, about 1½ hours. Gently run sharp knife around edge of pan. Cool completely in pan on rack. Refrigerate in pan at least 24 hours before serving or frosting.

White Chocolate Cream Cheese Buttercream

6   ounces white chocolate
1   (8-ounce) package cream cheese, at room temperature
½   cup unsalted butter, at room temperature
3   tablespoons fresh lemon juice

Break the chocolate into squares and place in the top of a double boiler set over very hot water on low heat. Remove double boiler from heat and stir until the chocolate is melted. Allow to cool. In a mixing bowl beat the cream cheese until smooth and creamy. Gradually beat in the cooled chocolate until smoothly incorporated. Beat in the butter and lemon juice. Allow cheesecake to come to room temperature before frosting. Store frosted cheesecake in the refrigerater.

Lemon Mousse Cheesecake

This cheesecake is so lemony and cool tasting that it is perfect for summer entertaining. Allow time for making ahead and freezing.

1¼ cups vanilla wafer crumbs (about 43 wafers)	1½ cups sugar, divided
¼ cup sugar	⅓ cup all-purpose flour
4 tablespoons unsalted butter, melted	6 egg yolks
	¾ cup fresh lemon juice
3 (8-ounce) packages cream cheese, at room temperature	4 egg whites, room temperature
	1 tablespoon lemon zest, chopped
	Confectioners' sugar

Butter a 9 x 3-inch springform pan and wrap the outside with a double layer of heavy foil. Preheat oven to 325°F. Crush wafers in food processor. Pulse in sugar and butter. Press crumbs in bottom of pan.

Beat cream cheese in mixer until fluffy. Gradually add 1¼ cups sugar, mixing until light and fluffy. Mix in flour and egg yolks. Beat for 1 minute. Slowly mix in lemon juice.

In a separate bowl and with clean beaters, beat egg whites until foamy. Gradually add remaining ¼ cup sugar, beating until stiff peaks form. Fold whites and lemon zest into the cream cheese mixture. Pour over crust and smooth the top. Place pan in a shallow roasting pan and place in oven. Pour about 1 inch of hot water into roasting pan. Bake for 55–65 minutes or until top of cake is well puffed and golden. Remove pan to a rack and let cool to room temperature. The cake will sink as it cools. Cover with plastic wrap and freeze overnight before serving. Cake can be frozen for up to 2 months. Cut cake with a sharp knife while frozen, dipping knife into hot water and wiping it clean before cutting each slice. Defrost overnight in the refrigerator. To serve, sift confectioners' sugar over the top. Makes 12 servings.

Chocolate Pots de Crème

I have a friend who has a set of porcelain pots de crème forms, complete with lids. What fun to lift the lid and find a small serving of the richest dessert imaginable. Even though they taste just as good in a ramekin, the pots are more fun.

1   cup heavy cream
¾   cup milk
12   ounces bittersweet or semi-sweet chocolate
6   large egg yolks
1   tablespoon Kahlua, optional

In a small saucepan, heat the cream and milk just to the point when small bubbles form around the edge of the pan. Break chocolate into pieces and place in the top of double boiler set over an inch of very hot, not boiling, water. Stir often until melted. Whisk in the yolks. The mixture will thicken. Gradually pour the hot cream mixture into the chocolate mixture, whisking constantly. Increase the heat so that the water in the bottom section of the double boiler simmers and, whisking constantly, cook for about 3–4 minutes or until thermometer reads 160°F. Remove at once from the heat and transfer to a metal bowl. Add the optional Kahlua.

Set the bowl over a larger bowl containing ice water and cool, stirring constantly with a rubber spatula, about 4–5 minutes or until room temperature. Divide the mixture among 8 pots de crème forms or ramekins. Cover with plastic wrap and refrigerate for at least 6 hours or up to 2 days. Makes 8 servings.

Persimmon Pudding

This persimmon pudding recipe is lighter than most Hoosier versions.
Baking the pudding in individual serving dishes makes this homey dessert
company fare.

⅓ cup plus 1 tablespoon all-purpose flour	1 cup frozen persimmon pulp, thawed
½ cup sugar	1 large egg
½ teaspoon cinnamon	2 large egg yolks
⅛ teaspoon salt	½ cup heavy cream
¼ teaspoon baking soda	⅓ cup milk
¼ teaspoon baking powder	½ cup pecans, chopped

Preheat oven to 275°F. Grease four 6-ounce soufflé dishes. In a large bowl, combine the flour, sugar, cinnamon, salt, baking soda, and baking powder and mix well.

In another bowl combine the persimmon pulp, egg, egg yolks, cream, and milk, and whisk until smooth. Add the dry ingredients and stir until smooth. Divide the mixture among the prepared dishes and top with the pecans. Place the dishes in a shallow baking pan. Balance the pan on the edge of the oven rack and carefully pour enough boiling water into the pan to reach halfway up the sides of the dishes. Bake until the pudding has risen and cracked slightly on the surface, about 40 minutes. (A tester inserted into the center will come out moist but not wet.) The pudding should not be firm. Using a metal spatula, transfer the dishes from the water bath to a wire rack and let stand at least 1 hour before serving.

(The pudding can be made a day ahead. Let it cool completely and keep covered in the refrigerator.)

Serve the pudding slightly warm. If cold, reheat it at 275°F about 8 minutes (or less, if the pudding has been held at room temperature). Serve with a dollop of whipped cream (flavored with a bit of cinnamon and sugar, if desired) or a scoop of vanilla ice cream, if desired. Makes 4 servings.

Orange Slices with Cinnamon, Brown Sugar, and Candied Ginger

The minced candied ginger gives the sweetened oranges added sweet heat. These are great after a Chinese dinner with an Almond Madeleine.

6   navel oranges
¼   cup firmly packed light brown sugar
1   teaspoon ground cinnamon
1   tablespoon minced candied ginger

Peel oranges and remove the white pith. Cut into ½-inch slices and arrange the slices side-by-side on a serving platter. Combine the brown sugar, cinnamon and candied ginger and sprinkle over the oranges. Let set for 15 minutes and serve. Makes 6 servings.

Raspberry Cabernet Sauce

When we were asked to cater a dinner for Hillary Clinton, we made this sauce and served it with individual coeur à la crèmes with mixed berries and mint. Imagine making this sauce using a full case of wine! During the final reduction we had customers swooning in the store. Even though Mrs. Clinton cancelled her appearance at the last moment, the dinner was a success. Being asked to cater that dinner has been one of the highlights of our business.

1   (750 ml) bottle reasonably good cabernet sauvignon or other red wine
1   cup sugar
12 ounces frozen raspberries, defrosted
½   teaspoon freshly ground black pepper

In a large, heavy, nonreactive saucepan or sauté pan, combine wine, raspberries, sugar and pepper. Bring to a vigorous boil over high heat and cook until it reduces to 2 cups, about 30 minutes. As sauce begins to thicken, stir with a spoon to prevent scorching. Strain liquid to remove seeds. Cool to room temperature. Sauce is wonderful on homemade ice cream, fruit, coeur à la crème, and cake. Makes about 1⅔ cups sauce.

Sautéed Strawberries with Basalmic Syrup and Amaretto

Tim McGrath, a guest chef from California, taught a superb class about sautéeing. He proved to us that good strawberries could be even better by sautéeing and adding balsamic vinegar. Small berries, consistent in size, work best for this recipe.

2   pints strawberries
2   tablespoons unsalted butter
½   cup aged (12 years) balsamic vinegar
¼   cup Amaretto liqueur
1   quart best quality vanilla ice cream
6   whole strawberries
6   sprigs mint

Wash and hull the berries, and place on paper towels to dry.

Heat a large sauté pan over medium heat and add butter. When butter has stopped bubbling, add strawberries. Sauté for 2 minutes, stirring briskly. With a slotted spoon, remove berries to a platter. Return pan to heat and add balsamic vinegar. Cook over high heat for 3–4 minutes. Drain any additional juices from strawberries on the platter back into pan. Add Amaretto and cook for an additional 2 minutes. Remove from heat and let cool for 5 minutes. Return strawberries to pan and stir. To serve, spoon over ice cream and garnish with mint and whole strawberries cut into fans. Makes 6 servings.

Charlotte Russe

For years I made this dessert at holiday time because of the raspberry sauce and the excuse to use a charlotte mold that had been given to me by a good friend. I don't know why I don't make it more often as it contains both custard and raspberries, two of my favorite tastes.

12   to 16 ladyfingers, split in half
4   large egg yolks
½   cup sugar
1   cup milk
1   2-inch piece of vanilla bean, split
2   teaspoons unflavored gelatin
½   cup chilled sour cream
½   cup chilled heavy cream
     Quick Raspberry Sauce (recipe follows)

Trim ladyfinger halves, tapering slightly at one end. Arrange these on the bottom of a 1-quart charlotte mold or soufflé dish with tapered ends meeting in center. Stack remaining ladyfingers, curved side out, around inside of the mold.

Soften the gelatin in ¼ cup cold water. Beat the egg yolks briefly. While still beating add sugar gradually. Continue to beat until mixture is thick and pale yellow. Warm milk and vanilla bean over moderate heat until bubbles appear around the edges of the pan. Remove the bean and slowly pour the hot milk into the eggs, beating constantly. Cook over low heat, stirring constantly, until the mixture thickens into a custard heavy enough to coat a spoon. Do not let it boil or it will curdle.

Remove the custard from the heat and add the gelatin, stirring until completely dissolved. Strain the custard through a sieve. Whip the sour cream and heavy cream together until stiff peaks form. Fill a large pot half-full with ice cubes and add water to cover by about 2 inches. Set the bowl of custard into the pot and stir with a metal spoon for at least 5 minutes or until it thickens to a syrupy consistency. Pour the mixture into the mold, smooth top with a spatula, cover with plastic wrap and refrigerate until set, about 5 hours. Unmold onto a plate, slice and serve with Quick Raspberry Sauce. Makes 6–8 servings.

Quick Raspberry Sauce

2   (12-ounce) packages frozen raspberries, thawed and drained
2   tablespoons sugar
1   tablespoon Kirsch or cherry brandy or lemon juice

Press the berries through a fine sieve to remove the seeds. Stir in sugar and liqueur or lemon juice.

Key Lime Mousse

⅝   cup key lime juice (5–6 key limes)
1   (14-ounce) can sweetened condensed milk
1   cup heavy cream

Slice limes in half and squeeze the juice into a medium bowl. Pour in the condensed milk and beat until smooth. Whip heavy cream until soft peaks form and fold into mixture. Pour into 4 glass containers, top with thin, twisted lime slices, if desired, and serve. (This dessert can be chilled or frozen until serving time. In a pinch, an 8-ounce container of whipped dessert topping can be used instead of the heavy cream.) Makes 4 servings.

Cinnamon Ice Cream

This is an ice cream flavor unavailable at the grocery. It is wonderful with chocolate of any kind. With the new no work ice cream machines, making it is easy.

3	cups heavy cream
1	cup milk
¾	cup sugar
1	whole vanilla bean, split in half lengthwise
2	teaspoons ground cinnamon
4	egg yolks

Heat cream, milk, sugar, vanilla bean, and ground cinnamon in a heavy saucepan over medium-low heat, stirring occasionally, until sugar dissolves and mixture is hot. Remove from heat. Remove vanilla bean carefully and scrape seeds from the bean back into cream mixture. Whisk egg yolks in a bowl. Slowly add 1 cup of cream mixture into yolks, whisking constantly until smooth. Slowly pour egg mixture back into cream mixture, whisking constantly. Place saucepan back over medium heat; stirring constantly, cook for 10–15 minutes, until mixture thickens. Do not boil. Pour through a fine strainer into a bowl. Chill to form a custard. Pour custard into bowl of ice cream maker and freeze according to manufacturer's directions. Makes 1 quart. Serve garnished with cinnamon sticks, if desired.

Cranberry Streusel Coffee Cake

Try to remember to put some bags of cranberries in your freezer so you can have this coffee cake year round. The cranberries add just the right amount of tartness to the sweet cake.

2½	cups all-purpose flour	1	teaspoon vanilla
1	teaspoon baking powder	1	tablespoon orange zest, grated
1	teaspoon baking soda	2½	cups fresh cranberries
½	teaspoon salt	¾	cup light brown sugar, packed
½	cup unsalted butter	2	teaspoons cinnamon
1	cup sugar	4	tablespoons unsalted butter
1	cup sour cream	½	cup walnuts, coarsely chopped
2	eggs		

Preheat oven to 350°F. Butter and lightly flour 9 x 13-inch pan. In a food processor with a metal blade, pulse 2 cups of flour, baking soda, baking powder and salt to mix. Remove to a bowl. Cream ½ cup butter with the sugar in food processor until light and fluffy. Beat in eggs one at a time. Pulse in sour cream and vanilla. Spread dry mixture evenly over batter in processor bowl. Pulse just until blended. Spread batter evenly in prepared pan. Sprinkle cranberries over the top.

Prepare streusel topping by tossing the brown sugar, remaining ½ cup flour, and cinnamon together. Cut in 4 tablespoons butter until mixture is crumbly. Stir in walnuts. Sprinkle mixture evenly over cranberries. Bake until tester inserted into center of cake comes out clean, about 45 minutes. Serve warm or at room temperature. Makes 10–12 servings.

German Apple Cake

This torte-type cake is one of the few desserts my son ever requested. It is good at breakfast or anytime you crave an apple dessert. Because it slices neatly it makes a nice tea time sweet.

1	cup sugar
1	cup all-purpose flour
4	tablespoons unsalted butter, cold and cut into 4 pieces
1	teaspoon baking powder
1	teaspoon vanilla
1	large egg
4	large Granny Smith or Jonathan apples

3	tablespoons sugar
3	tablespoons melted butter
1	teaspoon cinnamon
1	large egg

Preheat oven to 350°F. In food processor bowl with metal blade, process first 6 ingredients until mixture resembles coarse meal. Spread mixture in bottom of well-buttered 9-inch springform pan. Peel and slice apples and arrange in layers on top of the crumb mixture. Bake for 45 minutes.

Meanwhile, mix sugar, butter, cinnamon, and egg until smooth and sugar dissolves. Spoon mixture over apples and bake 25–30 minutes or until top is firm.

Key Lime Pudding Cake

Commercial key lime juice is readily available, making preparation of this dessert easy.

3	tablespoons unsalted butter, at room temperature
1½	cups sugar
4	eggs, separated
6	tablespoons all-purpose flour
	Pinch of salt
2	cups whole milk
⅔	cup key lime juice
	Fresh berries or thin lime slices

Preheat oven to 325°F. Lightly butter eight 6-ounce ramekins or custard cups. Cream the butter and sugar together to form a crumbly meal. Add the egg yolks one at a time, beating well after each addition.

Stir together the flour and salt in a small bowl and add to the creamed mixture in batches, alternating with the milk. Blend until the mixture is smooth. Add the lime juice, mix in well and set aside. Beat the egg whites until they form firm moist peaks. Fold them into the reserved batter, incorporating them thoroughly. Spoon the mixture into the prepared ramekins and place them in a shallow baking dish. Pour hot water into the dish to reach halfway up the sides of the ramekins. Place the baking dish in the oven and bake until the tops are lightly browned and springy to the touch, about 25–30 minutes. Remove the ramekins from the water bath and allow to cool. Serve warm, at room temperature, or chilled, topped with a berry or a thin lime slice. The cakes can be chilled and then unmolded onto serving plates. Makes 8 servings.

Raspberry Frangipane Cake

This cake can be simply decorated with a sprinkling of confectioners' sugar or drizzled with raspberry sauce for a more formal presentation. It is very rich because of the almond paste, so count on small servings.

7	ounces almond paste	1	teaspoon vanilla
14	tablespoons unsalted butter, softened	5	eggs
1	cup plus 2 tablespoons sugar	1	cup sifted cake flour
		1½	cups whole raspberries

Preheat oven to 350°F. Butter and flour a 9-inch cake pan which has been lined with parchment on the bottom. With a food processor or mixer with the paddle attachment, cream the almond paste, butter and sugar until smooth and light. Add the vanilla and eggs, beating well and scraping down the sides of the bowl. By hand, gently fold in the flour until the batter is just barely combined. Fold in the raspberries. Avoid overmixing or the cake will be tough. Pour the batter into the prepared pan and bake until the top is nicely brown and a tester inserted in the center of the cake comes out clean, about 50–55 minutes. Cool completely before removing from the pan. Serve cake plain or with a pool of raspberry sauce. Cake can be cut into two layers and filled with whipped cream and whole berries. Makes 12 servings.

Raspberry Sauce

2 cups raspberries, fresh or frozen
3 tablespoons water
¼ cup sugar
Lemon juice to taste

Sieve berries through a fine strainer to remove all seeds. In a small saucepan, combine the water and sugar and bring to a boil. Cool and add the raspberry puree. Add just enough lemon juice to brighten flavor. Store in refrigerator for up to one week. Stir well before using. Makes about 1¼ cups.

Desserts

Strawberry Shortcakes with Hot Cream Sauce

On one of our trips to the Napa and Sonoma areas of California we stopped at the Boone Hotel for lunch and had this dessert. I later read that Julia Child had this dessert also and went straight into the kitchen for the recipe. I didn't have the nerve to do that, but I did come across the recipe several years later. Enjoy it as we did.

2	cups all-purpose flour	¾	cup half-and-half
¼	cup sugar	2	cups heavy cream
1½	teaspoons baking powder	¼	cup sugar
¼	teaspoon freshly grated nutmeg	¼	cup unsalted butter
¼	teaspoon salt	2	pints strawberries, hulled and halved
½	cup unsalted butter, room temperature		Fresh mint
1	large egg, lightly beaten		

Preheat oven to 400°F. In a large bowl, mix flour, sugar, baking powder, nutmeg and salt. Add the butter and blend with a pastry blender until mixture resembles coarse meal. Place the egg in a 1-cup measure and add just enough half-and-half to make 1 cup. Slowly add to flour mixture, stirring with a fork. Do not overwork dough. With a spoon, drop the dough onto an ungreased baking sheet in 6 equal mounds. Bake for 10–12 minutes.

In a large saucepan over low heat, combine the cream, sugar and butter. Bring to a simmer and cook gently, stirring frequently, for about 30 minutes, until thick. Watch carefully, as mixture tends to boil over. Split the hot shortcakes in half. Place the bottom halves on 6 plates and top with the strawberries and the shortcake tops. Ladle the sauce on top, garnish with mint, and serve. Makes 6 servings.

Chocolate-Chocolate Bread Pudding

This recipe is a chocoholic's dream. Don't omit the whipped cream as it softens the intensity of so much chocolate.

2	tablespoons unsalted butter, melted	1	cup melted milk chocolate
4	large eggs, lightly beaten	6	cups cubed day old bread
1	cup firmly packed dark brown sugar	12	ounces bittersweet chocolate
3	cups heavy cream		White Chocolate Sauce (recipe follows)
1	cup milk		Whipped cream
1	teaspoon vanilla extract		Fresh mint leaves
½	teaspoon cinnamon		Confectioners' sugar
			Cocoa powder

Preheat oven to 350°F and grease twelve ½ cup muffin tins. In a mixing bowl, whisk together the butter, eggs, sugar, cream, milk, vanilla, cinnamon, and milk chocolate. Fold in the bread cubes and spoon ½ cup of the mixture into each muffin tin. Cut or break bittersweet chocolate into 12 cubes and press a chocolate cube into the center of each pudding. Bake for 35 minutes or until the puddings are set. Invert puddings and place each on a plate; drizzle with White Chocolate Sauce, and garnish with whipped cream and a dusting of confectioners' sugar and/or cocoa powder. Makes 12 servings.

White Chocolate Sauce

8 ounces white chocolate, chopped
1 cup heavy cream

In the top of a double-boiler over simmering water, whisk the chocolate and cream until sauce is combined well. Do not let the mixture overheat. Makes 1½ cups sauce.

Flan

This is one of my favorite recipes to serve with Tex-Mex food. It is rich but still very light.

¾   cup sugar
4   eggs
1   (14-ounce) can sweetened condensed milk
1   cup water
1   teaspoon vanilla

Melt sugar in a heavy skillet over low heat until sugar melts and turns golden. Pour into a 1-quart baking dish and turn dish to coat bottom and sides. Let cool.

Preheat oven to 350°F. Beat eggs and add sweetened condensed milk, water and vanilla. Pour into caramel coated casserole. Place casserole in shallow pan containing 1 inch of hot water. Place in oven and bake 1 hour or until a tester inserted into center comes out clean. Cool completely and chill before serving. Use a spatula along edge of flan to loosen. Turn out on serving dish and pour caramel over flan. Decorate with fresh fruit, if desired. Makes 6–8 servings.

Fat-free Raspberry Soufflé

For a while everyone seemed preoccupied with eliminating as much fat from their diets as possible. This dessert is certainly one you can enjoy if you are concerned with too much cholesterol. Serve this soufflé with a raspberry sauce and some fresh raspberries.

1   cup sieved good quality raspberry jam
1   tablespoon Grand Marnier, kirsch or liqueur of choice
6   egg whites, at room temperature

Preheat oven to 350°F. Prepare six 6-ounce soufflé dishes by spraying with vegetable spray and coating with sugar. Set aside. In a large bowl, whisk together the jam and liqueur until smooth. In the bowl of an electric mixer or with a whisk, beat the egg whites to soft, mounding peaks. Fold the beaten egg whites into the jam mixture until just combined. Fill soufflé dishes and level off the top. (This may be done up to 1 hour before baking. If so, cover the uncooked soufflés with plastic wrap and refrigerate.) Place the soufflés on a baking sheet and bake in the center of the oven until the tops have risen and are golden brown, 10–15 minutes. Serve immediately. Makes 6 servings.

About

Cooks & Company is a unique gourmet store located on Washington Street in Columbus, Indiana. The owners, Marie and Larry Huntington, have been active in Columbus' revitalization of its downtown area, and their store has served as an example to other area retailers and service organizations. In 1995, Cooks & Company was nominated for Business of the Year in conjunction with the State of Indiana's Main Street Program.

Shortly after her arrival in Columbus from California, Marie began teaching cooking classes. In September 1979 she and Larry began their retail business and have developed a multifaceted store that sells quality cookware, select packaged gourmet foods, and fine wines. Marie's cooking class repertoire now includes healthful cooking, Mediterranean, French, and Italian cooking, and pastry making. She and accomplished guest chefs from across the country offer over seventy-five classes a year.

Cooks & Company also features carry-out lunch items daily from a deli case that offers soups, sandwiches, salads, and desserts. Marie and her staff keep busy catering various private and corporate affairs, and the business is popular also for its special wine-tasting dinners.

Index

Index

Index

Index